LOVE,
SERVICE,
WISDOM

Cover design by Adrian Morgan
Cover art by drpnncpp | iStockphoto
Print book interior design by Frame25 Productions

Hierophant Publishing
San Antonio, TX
www.hierophantpublishing.com

If you are unable to order this book from your local bookseller, you may order directly from the publisher.

Library of Congress Control Number: 2025944655

ISBN: 978-1-950253-67-8

10 9 8 7 6 5 4 3 2 1

LOVE, SERVICE, WISDOM

The Ancient Inka Path to Inner Harmony

JORGE LUIS DELGADO

Hierophant publishing

To all the beings with whom we share this wondrous planet.

Contents

A Note on Quechua and Aymara Spellings ix

Introduction 1

Part One: Munay—The Path of Love

1. Awakening the Inner Sun 25

2. Love in Sacred Relationships 49

3. Sending Love Through Time 71

Part Two: Llankay—The Path of Service

4. Sacred Service in Everyday Life 93

5. Service in Sacred Relationships 117

6. Self-Care as Sacred Service 137

Part Three: Yachay—The Path of Wisdom

7. The Wisdom of the Three Worlds 161

8. Wisdom Beyond the Mind 183

9. The Wisdom of a Chakaruna 203

Conclusion 227

Glossary of Quechua and Aymara Terms 229

Acknowledgments 235

A Note on Quechua and Aymara Spellings

Quechua and Aymara, two of the indigenous languages in Peru and Bolivia, were widely spoken but had no written versions. When these languages were first recorded by Spanish colonizers and later by linguists, spellings varied widely. To this day, there is no single standardized spelling that is universally accepted across all Quechua- and Aymara-speaking places. Words may be spelled differently depending on the region, the dialect, and the transcription system being used. For example, you may see the Quechua word for organic energy spelled *kawsay*, *causay*, or *kausay*. Similarly, the Andean concept of sacred reciprocity might be written as *ayni* or *aini*. Throughout this book, when multiple spellings exist for the same word, I have generally used the one I grew up with. I have also included a glossary of common Quechua and Aymara terms at the end of the book.

Introduction

My name is Jorge Luis Delgado. Among my people, I am known as a *chakaruna*, or "bridge person." A chakaruna is one who helps others to "cross from one side of the river to the other": in other words, from one state of consciousness to other states of consciousness. A chakaruna can also form a bridge from the mind to the heart and from the present to the past or future.

Chakarunas travel their path quietly. They do not call attention to themselves, but offer their services in a variety of ways, such as through ceremonies and teachings that help people connect to their own divine nature. At the deepest level, a chakaruna is one who can walk between worlds. In my view, everyone has the power to connect to the divine in this way, and the only magic powers we need are the love, service, and wisdom we carry in our own hearts. By the end of this book, I hope that you, too, will understand your own potential to become a chakaruna and share the light of your inner sun with everyone you meet.

If you had told me when I was younger that I would someday write a book about Inka spirituality, I would have laughed. I was born in a small village near Lake Titicaca in Peru. My father was a schoolteacher, and my mother was a *yatiri*, a traditional healer. I grew up speaking Aymara at home, Quechua in the marketplace, and Spanish at school.

As a child, I wanted to be like my father: a rational, scientific, modern man. I was a little embarrassed by my mother, who seemed like she belonged to a different world, with her traditional handwoven cape and *chumpi*, always lighting incense and performing cleansing ceremonies in the house. The Aymara people have lived in the Andes for thousands of years, became part of the Inka civilization, and lived under Spanish rule until Peru declared independence in 1821. Although I was proud of my Aymara heritage, I was determined to follow in my father's footsteps, not my mother's.

Until I was six years old, my family lived in the countryside, where I could play outside and connect with Mother Earth every day. But when it came time for me to go to school, my mother took me and my siblings to live in the city. When I wasn't in school, my mother took me with her everywhere so I could help her make money for the family. We would go to the lowlands to sell wool or trade it for corn. From the lowlands, we would get some products and take them to the highlands on the weekends to trade. She taught me how to negotiate, and how to make a little profit by bringing a product from an area in which it was abundant to an area in which it was scarce.

As a child, I wasn't too interested in wool or corn, but I *was* eager to learn about business. I wanted to be the manager of a big company like the men I saw driving around in shiny cars in the city. It seemed to me that getting a Western education and achieving material success was the way forward in life. I certainly had no interest in my mother's prayers, rituals, and "backward" folk beliefs.

Then when I was eleven years old, the economy in Peru took a turn for the worse. I had to find a job so I could help pay for my younger siblings' school fees, uniforms, and even food. One day, I was walking the streets with an empty bag, looking for something I could buy and then sell at a profit. However, I only had one *sol* in my pocket—about thirty American cents. I spotted some kids running behind taxis, waiting to see where they would pull over. The moment one stopped in front of a hotel, the kids would open the trunk, pull out the passengers' suitcases, and carry the suitcases into the hotel in exchange for a few coins.

I stuffed my empty bag into my pocket and ran to join the other kids. The next time a taxi pulled up, I grabbed one of the suitcases inside. The passenger who owned the suitcase asked me, "How long have you been doing this?"

"This is my first day," I replied.

"Oh, really?" the man said. "How come?"

"Well, I'm just doing it for the experience," I bluffed, not wanting to admit that I needed the money because my family was poor.

The man gave me a huge tip. I was over the moon. I thought that from then on, I'd be rich. Of course, when I went back the next day, I discovered that most tips are much smaller—the man was just being kind because I'd told him it was my first time.

I started chasing taxis every day. Slowly, I learned a few words of English. Eventually, I figured out that I could get even more customers at the train station, so I would go there and act as a porter, guiding tourists to their hotels in addition to carrying their luggage. I was bringing home enough money that all of my younger siblings got to stay in school.

My mother insisted that all of my brothers and sisters finish school before going to work. As the eldest, I was the only one who was expected to drop out and support the family. I watched as one by one my siblings finished their educations and pursued well-paying careers. One of my brothers got a PhD in entomology; another became an engineer. I felt like they were leaving me behind, so in order to have something to show for myself, I began to study law at night. However, by that point I had been out of school for so long that I just couldn't settle into the rhythm of studying and taking exams. Instead, I decided to start a tour company of my own—after all, I'd been working with tourists for many years, and had become quite fluent in English.

When I first started out as a tour guide, I parroted the colonial history I'd been taught in elementary school. For example, the Spanish conquistadors assumed that the ancient ruins at Ollantaytambo were the remains of a military fort, so for years this is what I told my clients. Yet the more I educated myself about my people's history and culture, the more I learned about sites like these. Ollantaytambo was not just a fort, but a sacred site—home of the Sun Temple, whose stone altar is aligned with the path of the solstice sun, and of Intihuatana, an enormous sundial carved from granite.

The more I learned about Inka spirituality, the more I shared with the groups of visitors I led. I began to attract a different sort of clientele—spiritual searchers who were drawn to Peru for its sacred sites and power places. Unlike the tourists who came only to snap photos of Machu Picchu, these searchers wanted a deeper experience. They asked me questions about *munay*, *llankay*, and *yachay*, the sacred principles of love, service, and wisdom that form the core of Andean culture and spirituality. I even found myself guiding them through some of the cleansing practices my mother had taught me. Still, I reminded myself that I was just a tour guide, doing whatever would make the guests happy.

Then something strange happened. The guests who came on my excursions started giving me crystals from around the world. The first time it happened, I was touched but didn't think much of it. The second time, I thought it was a funny coincidence. Then one day, one of the visitors on my tour gifted me a two-inch-long amethyst shaped like a heart. When I carried this crystal around in my pocket, I began to feel a connection with Mother Earth unlike anything I had ever felt before. It seemed like the crystal had nudged me to a higher level of awareness, and opened my heart to energies I hadn't been able to feel before.

I began to seek out the traditional teachers and healers I'd ignored in my youth, and to finally learn the ways of my mother's people. The sacred sites to which I'd guided so many groups of tourists took on a new meaning for me, as I began to see them as living vessels of Inka spiritual wisdom. Many people believe that sites such as Machu Picchu, Lake Titicaca, and Sacsayhuamán are vortexes or "power spots" which the Inka people used to channel wisdom and spiritual energy from the divine. Indeed, the Inka people were remarkably knowledgeable about astronomy, and erected incredible stone structures to align with celestial events such as solstices and eclipses, drawing the energy of the heavens down to earth.

But what impressed me even more than the powerful energy at these sacred sites was the deep spiritual wisdom embodied in the Inka way of life. I realized that munay, llankay, and yachay weren't just beautiful concepts, but deeply practical principles for living a harmonious life on earth. Indeed, in our time of war, climate change, and dissolving social structures, they might just hold the key to *saving* the earth.

I decided to devote the rest of my life to studying this wisdom and sharing its gifts with others, and took my first tentative steps onto the path of the chakaruna. Today, I not only lead visitors to sacred sites in Peru, but I also write, speak, and teach workshops around the world, sharing the wisdom of the Andes with thousands of people every year—and I still carry my guests' suitcases whenever I get the chance.

The Inka civilization, known to its people as Tawantinsuyu or "the Realm of the Four Parts," stretched from the southern tip of modern-day Colombia to the southern tip of Chile, and thrived from about 1200 CE until its conquest by the Spanish in 1532. Although today the Inka people are most commonly associated with the high mountains, their territory included over five thousand miles of coastline, as well as rivers, lakes, and deserts. Thanks to their advanced technological skills, the Inka built magnificent cities such as Machu Picchu and Cusco, and supported a population of between six and fourteen million people with advanced agricultural systems based on terraces, canals, and aqueducts, which allowed them to grow and water their crops on steep mountainsides.

But while the Inka are rightly lauded for their achievements in architecture, art, and engineering, I believe their greatest contribution to humankind was their spiritual philosophy. Inka spirituality emerged from a deep understanding of our relationship with nature, the cosmos, and each other. The Inka understood that physical and spiritual realities are one and the same, that all aspects of life are sacred, and that we humans have both the power *and* the responsibility to create a state of harmony between the visible and invisible worlds.

Five hundred years after the collapse of the Inka civilization, and the subsequent suppression of Indigenous knowledge and traditions by the Spanish conquerors, this ancient wisdom is experiencing a resurgence. With stories of war, greed, and climate catastrophe confronting us at every turn, the Inka vision of a life characterized by harmony with nature, with other humans, and with the divine is more urgent than ever.

The New Era

The Inka people believe that time is characterized by thousand-year cycles, divided into two five-hundred-year *pachakutis*. In Quechua, the main language of the Inka which is still spoken by millions in the Andes, *pacha* means "time," while *kuti* means "turning" or "transformation." A pachakuti is a great turning—a time when old ways die out and a new way of living begins to take hold.

Some people believe that the year 1492 marked the beginning of a pachakuti characterized by conquest, destruction, and the suppression of the divine feminine. Over the course of five centuries, Indigenous cultures such as the Inka had their lands stolen, their children taken away, and their languages and traditional cultures outlawed. Wealth became concentrated in the hands of the few by extracting natural resources with the unpaid labor of the many. The earth suffered the scars of mining, deforestation, and the pollution of sacred waterways. Meanwhile, the dominant religions taught that humans were separate from nature, free to pillage it for their own gain while awaiting an afterlife in a distant heaven.

In Peru, the Spanish converted sacred Inka sites into churches and cathedrals, literally burying many masterpieces of Inka art and engineering under European-style spires and arches. Because the Inka people had no written language, the only "official" records of Inka spirituality from that time were written by the Spanish, with predictably distorted and sensationalized descriptions of sacred ceremonies and rites. Yet despite all this, Inka customs and traditions survived, passed down through oral tradition and often practiced in secret. This knowledge was like a handful of seeds that would someday sprout again, when conditions were right.

Now, the pachakuti of darkness is giving way to a new pachakuti characterized by wisdom, compassion, love, and awakening for all beings. Although the old pachakuti isn't giving up without a fight, as evidenced by a seeming increase in strife, oppression, and environmental destruction, these are merely the death throes of an era on the brink of extinction. As we enter the new cycle, more and more threads of light are making themselves known amid the darkness, and the wisdom of Indigenous peoples, including the Inka, is once more being celebrated and embraced around the world.

The Three Pillars of Inka Spirituality

Inka spirituality is based on three fundamental concepts: *munay* (love), *llankay* (service), and *yachay* (wisdom). However, the Inka understanding of these words is a little different from the English ones. Allow me to explain.

Munay means unconditional love for all beings and all experiences. Unlike romantic love, munay is not an emotion, but something akin to a cosmic force. The Inka people believe that munay is the energy that created, and continues to create, the entire universe. This kind of intense, all-encompassing love has the power to call things into being and manifest them on the physical plane.

When you practice munay, you live from the heart, approaching every moment of your life with tenderness and reverence, and recognizing your fundamental unity with all that exists. Everything is part of you, and therefore everything is worthy of your love. By practicing munay, we align ourselves with the power of creation, stepping from a place of separation or isolation into a life of unity where we are always in the flow.

Llankay means service, although it can also be translated as sacred work or sacred action. When we practice llankay, we align our actions with our highest values, so that everything we do becomes an act of service to the world. Whether you're planting a garden, writing a letter, or answering a customer's question at work, you can infuse your words and actions with care, awareness, and benevolence for all beings.

Llankay calls us to take a careful inventory of our actions in the world, asking ourselves if this action will push the world in the direction of greater harmony, beauty, and justice, or toward greed, conflict, and inequality. What message are we sending through our actions? What prayer are we making with our work? How can we make sacred service the central activity of our existence on earth?

Yachay means wisdom or discernment, particularly the wisdom that springs from recognizing your fundamental oneness with all that exists. It means recognizing that the same wisdom that lives in Mother Earth and Father Sun also lives in you; the wisdom of nature is not separate from the wisdom of humankind. In the Inka tradition, we acquire knowledge through love. This love gives us the ability to see clearly and discern the appropriate actions to take in any given moment.

All expressions of life contain wisdom—from stones, to waterfalls, to birds. To connect with this wisdom, we must slow down, open our senses, and observe things closely. By building our awareness in this way, we will find teachers everywhere—including within the depths of our own awareness.

Who This Book Is For

Now that we are moving into the new pachakuti, forms of knowledge that were once contained in a specific geographic area are now freely spreading around the world. Just as yoga was once unique to India but is now practiced nearly everywhere, Inka wisdom is likewise becoming accessible to millions of people who live far from the Andes. We are blessed to live in an age in which you do not need to live in Peru or speak Quechua or Aymara in order to benefit from the knowledge of the Inka people.

The problems currently facing humanity do not respect national borders. Catastrophes such as climate change, economic recessions, and a widespread crisis of meaning affect all people—and it is more important than ever that we share the tools needed to address them, rather than insisting that these tools be used only by a particular group of people. Although Inka wisdom has its origins in South America, it is applicable everywhere on Mother Earth. If you have ever yearned for greater harmony in your relationships, meaning in your work, and a deep sense of purpose in your life, this book is for you—whether or not you ever set foot in Peru. By practicing the principles of munay, llankay, and yachay, you can help humanity ascend from the heaviness and ignorance of the old era into the hope and brilliance of the new one.

Using the universal Inka principles of munay, llankay, and yachay, we can build bridges between things that may seem worlds apart: from the wisdom of nature to practices other modern humans can understand; from the earthly to the divine; from the mind to the heart; and from separateness to wholeness and peace.

The Inkas referred to themselves as "Children of the Sun" because they were acutely aware of the importance of this life-giving star: its rays melted the snow, warmed their bodies, and gave energy to the crops that sustained their lives. They knew that the energy of the sun lived in their own hearts, and that they were therefore eternal despite being mortal. This energy would live on long after they were gone, in their children and their grandchildren and on and on. We too can experience this kind of eternity in the present moment, bridging the fleeting experience of a human life with the scale of cosmic time.

Walking the path of the Inkas isn't just about personal transformation, but collective evolution. With munay in our hearts, we recognize the oneness of all life, and act with greater compassion for other people, animals, and Mother Earth. As we develop our capacity for unconditional love, we heal divisions, create community, and pave the way for reconciliation at every level of existence.

By cultivating llankay, we transform our everyday activities into humble acts of service for the benefit of all. We recognize that *every* action, no matter how small, unseen, or seemingly unnoticed, can contribute to the harmony of the universe when we perform it with conscious intention and love. Whether we're running a business, studying for a degree, or raising children, llankay teaches us how to infuse our activities with sacred purpose. With yachay, we build a bridge between our analytical minds and our intuitions, honoring both scientific knowledge and spiritual wisdom. We shift out of self-centeredness and learn to make decisions that benefit the whole, taking into account the needs of other people, creatures, and Mother Earth herself. Our "small mind" merges with the mind of the universe, infusing us with a vast and benevolent intelligence.

Ancient Inka prophecies speak of this time in history as a precious opportunity for humanity to awaken, turning toward our sacred relationship with Mother Earth and the wider cosmos. Walking the path of the Inkas isn't about turning back the clock and returning to a bygone era, but harnessing timeless wisdom to guide us into a better future. The problems humanity faces now can be our greatest teachers if we let them. The trauma and hopelessness can be our stepping stones to a golden age of harmony—and it all begins with individual people making a choice to put love, service, and wisdom at the center of their own lives.

The more we practice munay, llankay, and yachay, the more we summon these energies into the world—and the stronger the bridge becomes. This book is my way of inviting more people to join in the process of building this bridge. In the chapters that follow, we will delve deeper into the three pillars of Inka wisdom. Throughout, I'll offer exercises, ceremonies, and insights for incorporating Inka teachings into your daily life. Whether you're seeking healing, transformation, or practical ways to make positive change in the world, the ancient wisdom of the Inka people can be your guide.

As you establish munay, llankay, and yachay in your own life, you'll quickly discover that your relationships begin to change: not only with your friends, family, and coworkers, but with yourself, and with all of existence. Aspects of life that used to feel separate will begin to reveal their fundamental unity; you'll start to feel a greater tenderness toward all people, places, and experiences, knowing they are part of you. Perhaps best of all, you'll know that you're not alone, but are part of a vast network of like-minded people all working together to bring a new era into existence, for the benefit of all.

Part One

MUNAY
THE PATH OF LOVE

Chapter 1

Awakening the Inner Sun

In Peru, we say that munay is the energy that makes everything bloom—the flowers in your garden, but also your heart. This book focuses on the universal Inka values of munay, llankay, and yachay, or love, service, and wisdom. However, I could just as easily have written an entire book about munay, because love is always in service, and love is always wise. The most sublime, most profound aspect of life is love. It has a superior intelligence beyond our understanding, an intelligence that is not limited to human beings but that flows through all that exists.

When you embody divine love, you grow in sweetness, beauty, and wisdom. You give to others selflessly, the same way the sun gives warmth and the clouds give rain. If you only practice munay, you will naturally develop llankay and yachay, because munay is the quality from which all other qualities spring.

Nature is filled with munay. When you visit a tumbling waterfall, it offers its beauty to everyone, whether they are rich or poor, young or old. It doesn't ask for anything in return, but delights in its own existence. Similarly, the warm stones massaging your feet on a riverbank don't withhold their gifts from anyone, and neither do the ripe purple berries on a bush. Nature gives and gives, and in giving it reveals its full beauty, holding nothing back.

Mothers show munay toward their babies, feeding them and tending to them whether they are smiling or crying, and protecting them with a ferocity that can be surprising even to themselves. When we practice munay, we treat every creature on earth with a mother's warmth, tenderness, and care, welcoming them with open arms whether or not we find them beautiful or ugly, or pleasant or unpleasant to be around. We know that everything that exists is a manifestation of the divine, and that we have a role to play in that process of manifestation.

Munay is a beautiful way to live, elevating each moment of the day. Yet in the modern world we sometimes complain that loving others drains us. We get burned out from giving so much. We feel depleted after spending hours comforting a friend or helping our neighbors work out a solution to their conflict. We become codependent, taking on other people's emotions and problems, then put up emotional walls to make sure this exhausting situation can never happen again. How can we give like a waterfall or a river stone when this type of endless giving so often ends up leaving us feeling depleted? How can we practice true munay, which always replenishes us, instead of a love that drains? And, if love is such a wonderful way to live, why does it feel so hard sometimes?

Clearing the Obstacles to Love

In the Inka tradition, we say that the biggest barrier to practicing munay is *hucha*, or heavy energy. You see, in all of our relationships—whether with other people, with the experiences of life, or with ourselves—we sometimes carry things like resentment, guilt, or shame. These emotions weigh us down and drain our life force. Often, we're not even aware of the true cost of the hucha we're carrying in our lives. The way we feel seems normal to us, and so we're not aware that we're being weighed down by this heavy load.

One way to think about hucha is that it is anything that doesn't come from love. Most often, hucha manifests as fear: fear that you won't have enough, that you aren't good enough, or that you will be judged and found unworthy. Other times, hucha arises when we feel guilty about things we've said or done, or when we take on problems that aren't really within our power to fix or resolve. Hucha can also take the form of anger and resentment toward others, whether we're holding a grudge, placing blame, or still hurting from something someone has said or done.

Hucha can make you sick, both metaphorically and in some cases literally, affecting your physical, mental, and spiritual health. When you focus on the heavy experiences and emotions, endlessly repeating stories of unfairness and victimization, you hang out on a low frequency, which attracts more of those things into your life. This is true of habits like worrying as well. When you worry about a friend or family member, this might feel like love, but it's actually a form of hucha because it comes out of fear and generates more fear. When you gossip and commiserate as a way of feeling close with people, this might also feel like love—but all you're really doing is attracting even more hucha to the situation.

When we carry hucha, we starve our souls. You see, our souls need food just like our physical bodies. But the soul cannot digest hucha; it's like trying to eat stones instead of bread. When we feed ourselves these heavy energies—through harsh words, judgments, fears, and gossip, we create more and more hucha. It's like a garden where we keep throwing trash instead of planting flowers.

Often, when we have trouble practicing munay, when we feel burned out and depleted from sharing our love, it's because we have some hucha we haven't dealt with. For example, maybe we feel a tiny bit of resentment toward our friend even as we speak kind and comforting words to her, thinking to ourselves, *Why can't she just get it together? It's one crisis after another!* Or maybe we feel jealous of the love and support we're giving to others, wondering if anyone's going to come through for us the same way we're coming through for them. Instead of practicing true munay, we might mull over past trauma or calculate exactly what advantage we're going to gain by sharing our love, and this keeps us anchored to our hucha.

But you want to know something wonderful? Mother Earth knows exactly what to do with hucha. In the same way that she can take the food scraps we throw away and transform them into nutrient-rich compost, she can transform these heavy energies into light. Throughout the rest of this book, I'll give you many, many tools for releasing hucha so that Mother Earth can transform it for you. In Inka spirituality, we don't say that hucha is bad or negative—it's just heavy. Like compost in the garden, it may seem icky, but Mother Earth knows how to turn it into food for new life.

Another barrier to munay is the thinking mind, because we mostly use our minds to think judgmental and fearful thoughts, and this too attracts hucha. In the modern world, we are addicted to the mind. We think all day long, making future predictions, judging our circumstances in the present, or replaying the events of the past over and over. Unfortunately for us, all this thinking keeps us tethered to heavy energy. We think about bad things that happened to us, or about the bad things that might happen, and this feeds our hucha and makes it grow. Even if we want to practice munay, we say, "I have good reasons to be unhappy. This is a terrible world." In reality, all we're doing is feeding our heavy energy.

Finally, another very common barrier to munay is using cold words with ourselves. We say, *I'm not good enough*, *I'm not worthy*, *I should be smarter, faster, etc*. Every time you subject yourself to these kinds of judgments, you add to your stockpile of hucha. Not only that, but the more coldly you speak to yourself, the more likely you are to speak coldly to others, bringing hucha into your relationships.

How can we remove these barriers to munay from within our hearts? It's easy: by awakening our inner sun.

The Inner Sun

Most people on the planet today believe their main responsibility is to work. From the time we are children, adults are always asking us, "What do you want to be when you grow up? Will you be a doctor, a teacher, an engineer?" We feel proud the first time we earn a little money to bring home to our families, and for some of us, the ability to make money becomes central to our identity. We continue working long after our basic material needs are met, because that's the only way we know how to feel a sense of accomplishment, meaning, and pride.

But in reality, our most important responsibility isn't to work. Our most important responsibility is to remember the light. Everything alive on earth today came from the light, and this includes human beings. We came from the light, and we return to the light. Indeed, you could say that during our time on earth, what we are really doing is training for our return to the light. We are luminous beings and we are here to support life—to tend our beautiful Mother Earth, and to love each other. Yet many of us have forgotten this sacred task, or we never learned about it in the first place.

The most important task we have in this lifetime is to awaken our inner sun—the light in our heart that mirrors the light of the divine. You can think of the inner sun as a pure beam of light that has the power to transform anything it touches. It can lighten whatever is heavy, break down whatever is dense, and dissolve any experience that doesn't come from love.

This inner light that we can cultivate within ourselves is one and the same as the light of *Pachamama* and *Pachacamac*, the Cosmic Mother and Cosmic Father. The light that shines from Pachamama and Pachacamac has the qualities of clarity, warmth, transparency, and enthusiasm. When we awaken our inner sun, these qualities infuse our being as well. Let's look at each of them in a little more detail.

Clarity

Have you ever gotten up early to watch the sunrise? Have you ever noticed how the first light of early morning is so clear that you can see every detail of a flower, ocean wave, or blade of grass? It is this clear light that makes the birds sing at dawn, and causes the dew to rise up from the ground as steam. This clear light, which hides nothing while illuminating everything, is a good metaphor for munay: the love that literally makes the world go round.

When we are clear in our hearts, we are not easily led astray by things like greed, anger, and self-interest. We can see our past and future clearly, perceiving the events of our lives without exaggerating them or minimizing them. Instead of getting caught up in stories that may generate unnecessary hucha, we see things exactly as they are, and love them exactly as they are. We can also see ourselves clearly, and easily perceive when we are acting out of fear instead of love.

When we awaken our inner sun, we develop the power to bring clarity to any thought or situation. This quality of clarity clears away confusion and shows us the way to practice munay even under the most difficult of circumstances, just as Pachamama and Pachacamac share their munay with all of existence no matter what.

Warmth

Because Father Sun is warm, those who have awakened their inner sun are also warm. We express this warmth through our kindness to others, our generosity and hospitality, and the love that infuses our words and actions.

When you observe the sun's rays touching a flower, you can see how it responds: opening its petals, turning toward the light, growing taller and stronger. The sun doesn't force this response; it simply offers its warmth, and the flower naturally flourishes in its presence. Similarly, when our inner sun is awakened, people around us respond to our warmth without us having to demand their attention or manipulate them in any way.

A sure sign your inner sun has been awakened is when you begin using warm and loving words with both yourself and others, regardless of what the circumstances may be. Whether you are happy or disappointed, tired or refreshed, you nevertheless speak kindly, refraining from all forms of hostility, judgment, and blame. This warmth manifests not just in your words but in your tone of voice, your facial expressions, and even in your thoughtful silence.

In the Andean tradition, we believe that warmth is not just a pleasant quality but a healing force that can transform heavy energies into light. Just as the sun's warmth can melt ice into water that can quench our thirst and water our crops, the warmth of our inner sun can dissolve resistance, break through barriers, and forge connections. When we cultivate warmth in our hearts, we become natural healers in our families and communities.

Transparency

The light from the sun is transparent; it keeps no secrets, and hides nothing. Instead, it is constantly revealing itself, illuminating truths and showing its beauty in a million different forms.

In nature, transparency allows sunlight to penetrate water, revealing the darting fish, bright green algae, and other life beneath the surface. Transparency allows the sun's rays to filter through leaves, creating dappled patterns of shadow and light on the forest floor that delight our senses while allowing shade-loving organisms to thrive.

When we awaken our inner sun, we too become transparent. Instead of competing with others, playing games, or trying to gain an advantage, we are simple and guileless in our relationships. We say what we mean and mean what we say; we are honest with others and with ourselves. This quality of transparency makes life simple, clearing away the drama and complications that can arise when we keep secrets or pretend to be something other than what we are.

However, transparency doesn't mean we need to share every thought or feeling that passes through our minds. Rather, it means we don't intentionally mislead or manipulate others. We allow others to see our authentic selves, without the masks and defenses that separate us from genuine connection.

When we practice transparency, we discover that vulnerability is not weakness, but a profound source of strength and connection. Like a clear mountain stream that reveals every stone along its bed, we move through life with nothing to hide and nothing to prove.

Enthusiasm

Father Sun inspires leaves to unfurl, flowers to burst into bloom, and birds to sing in the treetops. Everything in nature seems to beam with happiness when the sun appears, and this includes human beings. Not only does the sun's warmth contain a great deal of energy, but it also awakens the enthusiasm for life in everything it touches. When mountain snows melt in the spring and summer, sleepy rivers wake up and start to babble and rush. Enthusiasm truly is contagious.

The word *enthusiasm* comes from ancient Greek roots *en* and *theos*, meaning "filled with God." This is precisely what happens when we awaken our inner sun: we become filled with the divine energy that animates all of existence. This enthusiasm isn't the frantic, nervous energy that comes from fear or ambition, but a deep, sustaining passion for life that wells up from within.

When you awaken your inner sun, you are curious, alert, and energetic, always ready to tackle new challenges or discover new things. Not only that, but your enthusiasm means you can see creative possibilities where others see dead ends. Just like the sun, your enthusiasm causes ideas, experiences, and relationships to flower, even in the most unexpected places. As if that weren't enough, the energy of your enthusiasm will resonate with others who are living at a similar frequency, meaning you easily attract people who share your vision, values, and goals.

In my tradition, we say that enthusiasm is a medicine for the hucha of apathy, self-doubt, and resignation. When communities gather for ceremonies or festivals, the collective enthusiasm generates a powerful energy field that can heal individuals and strengthen community ties. By cultivating enthusiasm in our daily lives, we contribute to this healing energy field and become carriers of the sun's revitalizing energy wherever we go.

Once you recognize the presence of your inner sun, and feel its beauty and luminosity within you, you begin to perceive the inner sun in other people, and indeed in all beings. And once you start perceiving the inner sun in all things, it becomes impossible not to regard them with munay. To some people, this sounds like too much—a romantic fantasy or an illusion. How can you really feel this tender, powerful, unconditional love for everything that exists? But we can do it. The moment you connect with your inner sun, you cannot help but realize that we are all rays of the same sun, of the same life. You cannot help but remember that we *are* love.

Cultivating Sámi

Just as we are capable of generating hucha, or heavy energy, we are equally capable of generating *sámi*, or refined energy. While hucha represents anything that doesn't come from love, sámi represents everything that *does* come from love. When we awaken our inner sun, our hucha naturally begins to drop away, and we begin to generate sámi instead. This is why awakening your inner sun is the most important thing you can do—not just for yourself, but for the planet, and for all of humanity.

When you constantly generate sámi, you are more likely to experience things like good luck, synchronicity, miracles, and blessings. You are more likely to make friends everywhere you go, and enjoy peace in your relationships. This is because sámi allows us to feel and reflect the harmony, clarity, and light within us.

One of the best ways to cultivate sámi is by enjoying the beauty of Pachamama. In English, Pachamama is often translated as Mother Earth.

However, Pachamama is more than the earth: she's our divine mother, our Cosmic Mother—the mother of the stars, the mother of time, the mother of the absolute. As long as we are alive, we have a strong connection from her heart to our heart. Her presence is always with us, teaching us the way of munay from the moment we are born.

Pachamama expresses her love through all of creation: mountains, stones, flowers, animals, the clouds in the sky, and the beautiful faces of the people around us. Pachamama does not withhold her love from us; rather, it is we humans who withhold our love from one another and from her, out of fear that we will not get enough, or that we are not truly worthy to possess what we already have.

When we look upon beautiful things, when we appreciate Mother Earth, we are feeding our souls sámi. When we pay attention to the munay expressing itself through the flowers and mountains, we realize that we too are expressing the beauty of nature. We realize that all of life is a manifestation of love. The more we look at life through that lens, the more we feed our soul, and the stronger our spiritual immune system becomes. We can shed hucha more easily; it doesn't hang around the way it used to. Just as Mother Earth breaks down old potato skins and chicken bones into compost, we can break down heavy energies like anger and regret, and turn them into pure munay we give to ourselves and others.

When you become aware that everything is alive and connected, you realize that everything you see is also seeing you. The highest level of consciousness is to realize that you *are* what you observe—the light that you see is a reflection of the inner sun that burns within you.

Exercise: Waking into the Light

In my lineage, the first thing we do every morning is remember that we are light. Every morning when you wake up, before you think about your job, the news, the economy, or your family troubles, go directly to your heart. With this practice, you activate the energy of munay, which will illuminate the rest of your day.

The moment you wake up in the morning, place your hand on your heart. Take a deep breath, and imagine your heart being filled with a warm, bright inner light. Stay here for several moments, feeling the light in your heart.

After you get dressed, go outdoors if possible. Facing east, open your arms wide toward Father Sun, with your palms facing up. Thank Father Sun for the life he has given you. Open yourself to receiving the light of the sun, even if it is hidden behind clouds. Feel the light spread all through your body, through all your cells, lighting up like little suns. Feel every cell in your body awaken to love, service, and wisdom. Allow yourself to remain in this state of connection until you feel your own inner sun blazing strongly within you.

Allow this light to guide your words, thoughts, and actions for the rest of the day.

Exercise: Loving Without Fear

In the Inka tradition, we say that the right hand is for giving, and the left hand is for receiving. We also use the right hand to pull in love and open the door of the heart, and the left hand to pull out hucha and close the door of fear. Whenever we give to others, we expand our love. And whenever we release heavy energies, the doorway of fear becomes smaller and smaller. I highly recommend this morning practice for establishing yourself in munay while letting go of hucha.

First, awaken your inner sun by doing the previous exercise.

Once you can feel the warmth and brightness of your inner sun, bring your right hand to your heart and your left hand to your solar plexus, at the top of your abdomen. With your right hand, you are giving love to yourself, and with your left hand you are closing the door of fear.

Stay here for a few moments, breathing in and out. Feel the door of fear getting smaller and smaller. Meanwhile, feel your capacity for love expanding. Notice your mind, body, and spirit coming into harmony with one another, and with the entire universe.

You can return to this practice several times throughout the day to balance your energy and anchor yourself in the energy of munay.

Chapter 2

Love in Sacred Relationships

Every moment you are alive, you are in a state of relationship. You are connected to Mother Earth, Father Sun, your blood family, your spiritual family, and your ancestors. Not only that, but you are also connected to the whole family of life: the plants, the animals, the insects, the birds, and every creature that drinks water, or what my people call the milk of the Mother Earth. All of these creatures are taking care of each other in a complex state of reciprocity.

Like many other Indigenous traditions, Inka spirituality emphasizes the importance of harmony in all your relationships. This is a reflection of the fact that we human beings are not isolated units, but part of a vast whole: what we do to others really is what we do to ourselves. If we dump poisonous chemicals where our neighbors live, they will someday seep into our own drinking water; and if we spread the heavy energy of gossip in our community, this energy will circle back to harm us as well.

The Seven Core Relationships

In my lineage, we say there are seven core relationships that every human being must tend to. These include your relationships with your mother, your father, your extended family, your community, the past, the future, and yourself. These seven relationships are critical to our physical, emotional, and spiritual well-being, so let's look at each one in a little more detail.

Mother

Our relationship to our mother includes not just our biological and/or adoptive mother, but Mother

Earth, the Cosmic Mother, and the divine feminine. During the last pachakuti, these sacred feminine energies were suppressed, as unbalanced masculine energy swept across the world. However, in this new era we are seeing a resurrection of the divine feminine—a quality that all humans can access within themselves, regardless of sex or gender.

In the modern world, many of us feel pain and guilt in our relationship with the mother. Either we've repressed the divine feminine within ourselves, denying ourselves beauty, tenderness, and receptivity, or we feel terrible for the ways our actions have harmed Mother Earth. We feel cut off from the Cosmic Mother who holds everyone and everything within her divine embrace. Carrying hucha in this relationship can make us feel lost, alone, and unloved, but when we have harmony in our relationship with the mother, we feel deeply nourished and we awaken to the ways we are constantly being showered with gifts.

Father

Our relationship to the father encompasses not only our biological father and/or the father who raised us, but Tata Inti, or Father Sun, as well as the Sun behind the Sun, the Cosmic Father, and the divine masculine. Even though we're entering a time when feminine energy is making a beautiful resurgence, we must still tend to the masculine as well. Both men and women must possess and harmonize the masculine and feminine energy inside themselves to develop munay, llankay, and yachay. The light of Father Sun brings vitality to our bodies, clarity to our thoughts, and a fierce protective spirit to our hearts.

If you are carrying hucha in your relationship with the father, you may feel a lack of energy, drive, and motivation—a sense that your inner sun is clouded over, and that you can't access its warming rays. Hucha in this relationship can also manifest as feelings of shame for the masculine qualities within yourself, or difficulty relating to the important male figures in your life. Clearing this heavy energy often means reconnecting with the positive aspects of masculinity, such as courage, strength, and self-reliance. When your relationship with the father is in harmony, you feel warm enthusiasm for life's challenges, and confident in your own abilities to meet them with grace.

Your Family

While your relationships with your family of origin may be complicated and perhaps fraught, it is important to tend to these sacred relationships. The Cosmic Mother and Father had good reasons for placing you in your particular family, even when those reasons are hard for you to see. Family is the vital nucleus of our identity, representing lineage and continuity. Often, our relationships with our families constitute the true test of our ability to express munay, llankay, and yachay.

Unless you were born into an extremely harmonious family, chances are you are carrying some hucha with at least one relative—whether it's the older sibling who tormented you during your childhood, or the grandmother who disapproved of your choice of a mate. Clearing hucha in these relationships often involves a lot of forgiveness, which we will discuss later in this chapter. Remember, our Cosmic Mother and Father chose our family members for a good reason—they are often our toughest teachers, and nurturing these relationships offers one of our greatest opportunities to grow. When our family relationships are in harmony, we feel a sense of security, gratitude, and pride.

Your Community

In Inka spirituality, community refers not just to your close neighbors and acquaintances, but to people in other cities and countries as well: the great community of humanity. In my tradition, we believe that all living beings are part of our community: plants, animals, minerals, mountains, bodies of water, and other expressions of nature. We should see all these expressions of life as our brothers and sisters, as we are all children of Father Sun.

Sadly, many of us today aren't aware of having hucha with our communities, because we don't realize we're in a community at all. Instead, we wave at our neighbors from across the street, content to keep a safe distance between us and them; we may notice the birds and butterflies when we go for a walk or hurry to our jobs, but we don't consider them our friends and family. In cases like this, the hucha that exists is the hucha of neglect. Even if we don't realize it, there is often a deep sorrow in the place where love and connection with our community is supposed to be. Clearing this hucha often involves slowing down, paying attention, and making that step to forge connections with the living beings around us. It may be awkward at first. You may not always feel validated or that your efforts are reciprocated. But when a genuine connection or exchange happens, it's all worth it. When your relationship with your community is in harmony, you feel a sense of recognition and belonging wherever you go.

Your Past

In the Aymara language, the word *nayra* means "the past," but it also means "eye." In other words, we *see* with the past. Our past is what shapes our perception and our worldview. Because it is associated with the eyes, the past is considered to be in front of us, not behind us. After all, we can see the past clearly because we already know what happened, unlike the future, which is unknown.

Just like the other sacred relationships, our relationship to the past can be characterized by hucha or by sámi. If you have suffered in the past, you may have lots of hucha which needs to be brought into the light. This heavy energy might manifest as regret, shame, or a tendency to replay old hurts and disappointments. You might feel trapped by painful memories, stuck in a victim mindset that suggests that your past experiences define who you are today. This hucha can keep you anchored to old patterns and prevent you from seeing new possibilities. Healing our relationship with the past is most powerful when we can extend forgiveness to ourselves, to others, and even to life itself. When you bring harmony to your relationship with the past, you learn to see and appreciate the gifts of your experiences, and share those gifts to lessen the suffering of others.

Your Future

Just as the past is in front of us, the Inka conceive of the future as being behind us. This is because the future is something we cannot see; it's still unknown to us. It's also because the unfolding of the future depends on how we position ourselves in front of the past and deal with it. However, the more work we do to clear our past of hucha, the more we can envision a bright and happy future, instead of dreading the days to come.

If you're carrying hucha in your relationship with the future, you might experience chronic anxiety or dread about what's to come. This heavy energy often manifests as a paralyzing fear that prevents you from taking productive action in your life. You might find yourself constantly worried about worst-case scenarios and unable to envision good possibilities. Clearing this hucha often means reconnecting to your inner sun, the source of light that will always be with you no matter what your future holds. When you have harmony in your relationship with the future, you feel a deep sense of trust in your ability to handle whatever comes, and feel a warm sense of excitement about the good things still to come.

Yourself

The seventh sacred relationship is with your inner self, your authentic self, your inner sun. If you don't establish a baseline of love, service, and wisdom in your relationship with yourself, it's impossible to establish, maintain, and project these qualities in your other sacred relationships. Do you like yourself and feel comfortable in your own skin? Do you speak warmly to yourself? Do you believe yourself to be good, because you know that you are inseparable from the innate goodness of life?

If you are carrying hucha in your relationship with yourself, you might engage in harsh self-talk, constant self-criticism, or feel fundamentally unworthy of love. This heavy energy can manifest as imposter syndrome, perfectionism, or a deep sense of shame about who you are. You might find it difficult to accept compliments, tend to dismiss your achievements, or constantly compare yourself unfavorably to others. When you carry hucha toward yourself, it ripples out into all of your other relationships—so it's especially important to transform this energy as soon as you realize it's there. When you have harmony in your relationship with yourself, you experience a deep sense of peace and unshakeable security, which is perceptible to the people around you.

If you think of your time on earth as a training period for your eventual return to the light, these seven relationships are your biggest teachers. If you struggle with one or more of these relationships, this might sound overwhelming—however, know that when you heal any single one of these relationships, all of them become stronger. When we tend the garden of one relationship with love, all the other gardens bloom. That's why it's so important to be aware of all our relationships—because they are not separate. They weave together to form the fabric of our lives.

Clearing Heavy Energy from Relationships

Chances are that you're carrying hucha in one or more of these relationships. While it's normal to experience some conflict from time to time, hucha accumulates in our relationships when we hold on to resentment, anger, jealousy, or fear. These heavy energies act like anchors, keeping us tied to past hurts and preventing us from coming into a state of harmony again.

The process of clearing hucha from our relationships involves four steps. I call these the Four Steps of the Condor, because just like the majestic Andean condor, they require us to fly high up, where we can get a wider perspective on our lives.

Step One: Acceptance

We begin by simply acknowledging that there is heavy energy present in the relationship. Instead of denying our feelings or engaging in wishful thinking, we honestly admit that something is off, and we do our best to name what it is. Is there anger? Guilt? Irritation? Boredom? Blame?

Step Two: Separation

Next, we separate ourselves from the situation to observe it more clearly. What are the larger patterns in play here? How does this experience tie into similar experiences in your life? What's the first time you remember feeling this emotion or having this kind of conflict?

During this step, we often discover how this heavy energy connects to other moments in our lives—we become aware of the patterns we keep on repeating and their roots.

Step Three: Revision

From this higher vantage point, you can begin to see the situation differently. You realize you are not the heavy energy—it's just something that has attached itself to you temporarily. Whatever conflict you're experiencing is just a lesson on your path, which will ultimately help you to expand your light.

Step Four: Transformation

In this final step, we recognize that all challenges are invitations to transform hucha into sámi. The argument you have with a parent can be a catalyst for greater love and understanding; the struggles you went through in the past can become the compassion you show toward others. The moment you see the experience as precious, *exactly as it is*, is the moment you transform the heaviness you're holding into light.

The Power of Forgiveness

Forgiveness is one of the most powerful ways we can clear hucha from our relationships. Inka spirituality teaches that forgiveness is a gift from the Cosmic Mother. No matter what we do, this mother is always there for us, ready to welcome us back into her loving embrace and surround us with the light of munay. We don't have to do anything to "deserve" or "earn" this forgiveness; it's always there, ever-flowing like a river.

With practice, we can learn to give the gift of forgiveness to ourselves and others the same way the Cosmic Mother gives it to us: freely, and with great tenderness. Forgiveness doesn't mean forgetting or condoning harmful actions—rather, it means releasing the hucha that keeps us bound to past hurts. Instead of looking at others through the lens of our past pain, we can see them through the lens of our inner sun, in which all experiences, no matter how difficult, reveal themselves as potential sources of healing, love, and light.

Forgiveness isn't just an intellectual exercise. Releasing heavy energy often requires ceremony and ritual—a way to bring our forgiveness into our bodies and into the physical world. For example, you might want to write down all of the harmful things a family member did to you, then burn the paper in a fire, or take a hike to the top of a mountain and create a ceremony in which you make a prayer of gratitude to the Cosmic Mother, thanking her for making your life exactly the way it is.

Gratitude and hucha cannot coexist, so if you're 100 percent grateful for your life, it means you have forgiven everything.

Forgiveness is one of the most liberating emotions we can feel, and practicing forgiveness provides us with an ever-rejuvenating source of spiritual vitality. If we cannot or do not forgive, we will continue to feel drained, because holding on to bad memories and painful stories distracts us from the beauty of life.

At its core, forgiveness means letting go of anything in your relationship that doesn't come from love. You just open yourself, and you are grateful. You feel this gratitude in your body, in all your cells, in your mind, and you can feel that the hucha is gone. What remains is light connecting you to all of existence, imbuing all of your relationships with the divine warmth of munay.

Exercise: Seeing the Light in Others

When you become aware of your own light and beauty, you realize that everything that exists is also in that same frequency. In this exercise, I invite you to make that discovery for yourself.

First, find a place to sit where you will see a variety of people walking by—for example, a park or shopping mall. Take a moment to connect with your inner sun, breathing in and out and imagining light flooding the cells in your body. Once you've established a strong connection within yourself, look around and let your eyes fall on the first person you see. Allow yourself to notice all the beauty in this person, whether or not they are conventionally beautiful. Look past outward appearances and see their inner light. Remember that they too are connected to the Cosmic Mother and Father.

Repeat this process with several people in the crowd. Notice how your heart becomes tender when you practice seeing strangers through the eyes of love.

Then repeat this process with different elements in your environment. Practice seeing plants, animals, and objects with love and tenderness. Once again, notice how your heart softens when you bring munay into your gaze.

There is no need to stop this exercise at any point. Instead, see how long you can maintain this practice—for hours, days, or even weeks. What would it be like if you *only* saw life through the eyes of love?

Exercise: Self-Assessment for Heavy Energy

At least once a year, it's good to sit down and take inventory of any hucha you may be carrying in your relationships. In this exercise, I invite you to sit down with a journal and brainstorm the answers to the following questions:

- How am I carrying hucha in my relationship with the mother?

- How am I carrying hucha in my relationship with the father?
- How am I carrying hucha in my relationship with my family?
- How am I carrying hucha in my relationship with my community?
- How am I carrying hucha in my relationship with my past?
- How am I carrying hucha in my relationship with my future?
- How am I carrying hucha in my relationship with myself?

After you've done your initial brainstorm, go back through your list and answer the following questions for each relationship:

- Do I use warm or cold words when thinking and speaking about this relationship?

- What heavy energies am I holding on to in this relationship (e.g., anger, resentment, fear, jealousy, guilt, blame)?
- What would this relationship look like if I could see it through the light of my inner sun?

Remember that bringing munay to your relationships is an ongoing practice. Each day offers new opportunities to clear hucha and choose love. When you do this work consistently, you will begin to experience all your relationships as sacred expressions of the divine light that connects us all.

Chapter 3

Sending Love Through Time

The Inkas believe that the universe mirrors back to us exactly the same energy we give to the universe. If we approach life with munay, we see love everywhere. If we approach life with negativity or cynicism, we find more things to criticize and complain about. As human beings, we must constantly be tending our energy, making sure we don't become unbalanced. We must also maintain a constant awareness of our relationships with everything that exists—including our ancestors who walked the earth in the past, and the generations of people, plants, and animals who are still to come.

One important way we tend our energy and our relationships is through the use of ceremony. Ceremony puts us in a state of harmony with ourselves and right relationship with the natural world. It helps each of us remember that we are Pachamama's caretakers, and it allows us to reaffirm our commitments to taking care of her so that future generations can thrive, just as our ancestors took care of her so that we could thrive.

One of the most important aspects of ceremony is that it dissolves our conventional notions of time and space. Within the context of ceremony, you can send love to ancestors who died many years before you were even born, and to great-great-grandchildren who will arrive many years after you die. You can send love to other parts of the world, to people you will never meet, and connect to the spirits of animals, plants, and mountains even if they are thousands of miles away.

In the previous chapter, we discussed the importance of bringing munay to your sacred relationships, including your relationship with the events of your past and the unknowns of your future. Now, I'd like to expand your concept of the past and future to encompass not only your personal experiences, but the vastness of history—both that which has already been recorded, and that which has yet to be written.

Sending Love to Your Ancestors

In ancient Peru, people believed that ancestors weren't gone, but could still watch, listen, and intervene in the affairs of the living—and in contemporary Peru, making offerings to one's ancestors is still a common practice. Our ancestors live inside us, in our blood and DNA; their love and wisdom can still guide us, if we take the time to love and remember them.

What does it mean to bring munay to the deep past? In some cases, this means forgiving your ancestors for the mistakes they made. Just as we've all taken actions out of ignorance that we later regret, our ancestors, too, had moments when they acted out of ignorance—times when they harmed other people, desecrated Pachamama, or allowed hucha to dominate their relationships.

Sometimes, we feel ashamed of our ancestors for their mistakes, and this shame becomes its own form of hucha, draining our energy and starving our souls of nourishment. We think, *They were terrible, they were ignorant, I can't believe they did those things.* Meanwhile, we forget that our ancestors are still living through us, and that we can purify their heavy energy through the positive actions we take in the present. The munay we cultivate in our own hearts travels through time, bringing light to everything it touches. Once you understand this, shame and anger toward your ancestors goes away.

Bringing munay to the deep past also means expressing gratitude for your ancestors' courage, self-sacrifice, and other positive qualities. It means reflecting on the hardships your ancestors overcame, the technologies they invented, the artwork they created, and the spiritual wisdom they passed down. Perhaps most important, it means opening your heart to receiving the incredible love your ancestors feel for you, and which they have been sending forward in time since long before you were born.

In the Andean tradition, we understand that our ancestors never really leave us. They are simply in another dimension, another state of being, but their energy and their light remain connected to ours. This is why when we visit sacred sites like Machu Picchu or the temples around Lake Titicaca, people often feel a sudden wave of emotion—they are feeling the presence of ancestors who walked these lands long ago. These ancestors are reaching across time to touch their hearts, sending them munay just as we send our munay to them.

Sending Love to Future Generations

Just as we can heal the deep past through the power of munay, we can also heal the future.

Many families have a terrible secret—a pattern like violence, depression, or addiction that is repeated generation after generation. Some people even believe that these heavy patterns persist for seven generations—seven generations of addiction, seven generations of depression or mental illness, and so forth. This belief is like a curse, condemning people to carrying that heavy energy. By tapping into the power of munay, you can purify this heavy energy in your own lifetime; you can cut this cord for the next generations and say, *No more.*

The first step in breaking these patterns is awareness. You must call on the qualities of clarity and transparency to see the pattern clearly, without denial or minimization, and also without exaggeration. Ask yourself: "What heavy energies have I inherited from my family? What stories keep repeating themselves?" Write these patterns down or speak them aloud, bringing them into the light of your inner sun.

Next, you must recognize that these patterns are not your fault, nor were they entirely the fault of those who came before you. Your ancestors did the best they could with the awareness they possessed at that time. When you truly understand this, the hucha of guilt, shame, and blame is transformed into compassion. The work you do to transform this ancestral hucha is your gift of love to future generations.

Another way to send love to the future is to treat Pachamama with reverence—restoring what has been desecrated and using only what is necessary to meet your basic needs. Whenever you plant a tree, you are sending munay to future generations who will someday stand under its shade. Whenever you feel happiness and contentment in your heart, without needing to buy anything or go anywhere, you are creating a world in which the children yet to be born can thrive.

In the modern world, we are often taught to focus on our own desires for beauty, success, and material comfort. In the midst of all this focus on the self, we forget about the costs to future generations, and as a result of this forgetting, our lives fall out of balance. The truth is, we have a sacred duty toward those yet to be born, just as our ancestors had a sacred duty to us. We are going to leave this earth behind for the next generation to live on, and it needs to be in good shape. Sending love to the future means tending Mother Earth in the present, and expressing our gratitude for all that she gives us every day.

You can also send munay to future generations by speaking to them in your heart. Many times when I take visitors to sacred sites in Peru, I invite them to sit quietly and open a conversation with those who will come after us. This isn't just imagination; when we speak from our inner sun, our words travel beyond the limitations of physical reality. You might say something like, "Beloved ones who will walk this earth when I am gone, I am working to heal the heavy energies of my lineage so that you may walk in greater light. I am caring for these waters, these mountains, and these plants so they will nourish you as they have nourished me. I am sending you my love across time."

Perhaps the most powerful practice of all is to live as if future generations are watching us right now—because on the cosmic level, they are. When you make choices in your daily life, ask yourself: "What would my great-grandchildren think of this decision? Would they thank me, or would they wish I had chosen differently?" This practice brings the future into the present moment, allowing us to feel the impact of our choices before we make them. Every time we choose love over fear, generosity over greed, and harmony over conflict, we are weaving threads of light into the fabric that future generations will inherit. This is munay in its highest form—love that extends beyond our own lifespan to embrace all of time.

The Importance of Ceremony

One of the best ways we can send love to the deep past and future is through ceremony. In my years as a tour guide, I've noticed that my North American guests love to learn about and participate in Andean rituals and ceremonies such as the *despacho* and the *k'intu*. They often tell me that life in the United States is focused on the mind: people read about spiritual subjects, but they don't quite know how to embody the beautiful ideas they read about in a tangible way. Ceremony helps us work with our energy, actively shedding hucha and generating sámi; otherwise, it's all intellectual, and nothing really changes.

Some spiritual teachers claim that they can show you the safe way to perform a ceremony, which implies that there is an *unsafe* way to do a ceremony. This has always bothered me, as it leads people to worry that ceremonies and rituals are dangerous and can have serious consequences if you make a mistake. This simply isn't true. All that matters is that you go into ceremony with an open heart, and participate using the purest part of yourself. If you do that, everything will be alright.

Before beginning any ceremony, it's always good to set your intention. Your intention puts you in direct contact with the world of possibilities—and with the Divine Mother, everything is possible. Intention springs from a strong conviction of will, infused with the munay that lives in your heart. A strong intention carries powerful energy that can cause even seemingly impossible outcomes to manifest into real life. Whether it's reconciling with a family member or preserving a mountainside for future generations, anything is possible when your intention is strong.

After you set your intention, take a moment to look around and appreciate where you are. Ask permission from Mother Earth and from the spirits of the land to perform your ceremony. This respectful attitude will help you enter into divine communion with the Cosmic Mother and Father.

The next step I recommend is to open sacred space. This consists of making one or more ritual gestures to indicate that you are stepping out of your ordinary way of speaking and being, and entering the realm of divine speech and action. Sacred space can be opened in a variety of ways. For example, you might burn fragrant herbs to cleanse and purify your energy, light candles, say a prayer, or call in the spirits from each of the four directions. Do whatever feels right to you that reflects the sincerity of your intention.

Once you've set your intention, asked for permission, and opened sacred space, the rest of your ceremony is up to you. In Peru, we often do a ceremony called a *despacho*, which means "to send." We use despacho ceremonies to send our gratitude to Mother Earth, to request healing for a physical or emotional ailment, to restore balance and harmony in our relationships, or to make a special request of the spirit world.

The ceremony includes making a small prayer bundle or sacred offering. This usually consists of things like flowers, coca leaves, feathers, and shells. We arrange these things beautifully so that Mother Earth feels loved, cared for, and respected by her children. Mother Earth feels us, breathes with us, and attends to all of our needs. If we conduct our ritual with munay, we can release our heavy energies with ease, because she knows how to transmute them into sámi, the energy of light.

Another ceremony we often do in Peru is the k'intu ceremony. *K'intu* means "offering" in Quechua. Traditionally, a k'intu consists of three coca leaves: one for the Apus, or mountain spirits; one for Pachamama; and one for humanity.

For the Inkas, coca is a sacred plant. Some people trace the origins of the word *coca* to the Aymara word *khoka*, which means "tree." Legend has it that Khuno, the god of storms, once set a huge fire that wiped out all the food crops, leaving only the coca plant; when the people chewed it, they discovered that it suppressed their hunger, gave them energy, and made them more resilient against the cold. Another legend says that Manco Capac, the founder of the Inka civilization, gave coca to the Inkas as a reward for their hard work. Yet another says that coca was a beautiful young woman whose seductions were causing so much chaos that she was sentenced to death. Her body was buried in the gardens of her many lovers, where she grew back in the form of the coca bush we know today.

To this day, Mama Coca is considered *huaca*, or sacred, to Andean people, who use it for divination, healing, and to communicate with spirits and ancestors. In the k'intu ceremony, we use the power of the breath to blow our prayers or our hucha into the bundle of sacred leaves, which we then give to Mother Earth to digest. In some cases, we first pass the k'intu over the three main energy centers in our bodies—the belly, heart, and head—for purification.

You don't have to live in the Andes or have access to coca leaves to do these ceremonies at home. In fact, it is a wonderful thing to create variations of these ceremonies using elements from your home environment. For example, maybe you don't have access to coca leaves, but there is another sacred plant such as mugwort that you can gather near where you live. Adapting ceremonies to reflect your local environment is a wonderful way to connect with Mother Earth and honor your own unique ancestry. If you live near the beach, you can use seashells and sand in your despacho; if you have Japanese ancestry, you might feel called to use a few leaves of *sencha* or a sprig of *sugi* in your rituals. Choosing items that reflect your own heritage can help you feel connected to the ancestors who came before you and the descendants who will come after you.

Practicing Love for All Beings

Of course, the more we practice sending love to the past and the future, the more we realize that we are connected to all beings, not just our immediate ancestors and real or potential progeny. If you go back far enough, we all come from the same ancestors; and if you go forward far enough, we all become related once again.

Munay does not discriminate or judge; it does not put one thing over another and establish hierarchies. Instead, it is respect and acceptance for all that exists. It is the divine aspect that we carry within ourselves. When we practice the virtues of gratitude, generosity, and compassion, or awaken these qualities through ceremony, that's when we touch the heart of munay in our own lives.

The best decision you will ever make is to love. Whether it's loving yourself, your family, future generations, Mother Earth, or all the creatures that inhabit her, the munay you cultivate will illuminate your life, dissolving all of the imaginary boundaries that keep you separate from the whole.

Exercise: Despacho Ceremony

To perform your own despacho ceremony, start by gathering a few small items such as candy, coins, rice, flowers, seeds, crystals, feathers, or shells—anything that you feel would be a valuable gift to Pachamama to express your gratitude for her gifts to you. You will also need a large piece of paper and a length of string.

Once you have gathered your items, open sacred space by lighting incense, making an invocation, or conducting whatever ritual feels meaningful to you. Place the piece of paper in front of you. Take your offerings one by one and say a prayer of gratitude for each as you place it on the paper. As you place your offerings on the paper, pay attention to the pattern you are making. Do your best to make a beautiful shape, like a mandala, instead of simply piling up the objects. Every time you add a new element to the despacho, explain why you are thankful. For example, if you're adding honey to the paper, you might say you are grateful for the sweetness of your life.

Once you have placed all of your gifts onto the paper, close your eyes and open your hands to receive the blessings from the despacho. Thank Pachamama for all she has provided to you. If you have a request for healing or assistance from the spirit world, now is the time to make it. Now fold the corners of the paper into the center to create a square bundle, being careful not to let any of your offerings spill out. Tie the bundle with string as if you are wrapping a present for Mother Earth.

As a final step, take your despacho bundle and burn it, bury it, or release it into water. You can also leave it on a mountain, at the base of a tree, or in another natural place, knowing the Apus, or spirits of the land, have received it.

Exercise: K'intu Ceremony

In the Andes, we perform a k'intu ceremony to release hucha and feed it to Mother Earth using coca leaves. If you don't have access to coca leaves, you can do the same ceremony using flower petals or herbs that grow in your area.

To start, take three leaves or petals and fan them in your hand to create a bouquet, with the stems pointing down and the leaves facing up. This bundle is a k'intu. Next, take a moment to gather your awareness of any heavy energy you wish to release. Bring your k'intu bundle to your belly and pause, feeling your connection to your ancestors, the people not yet born, and the root of your being. Now bring your k'intu to your heart and pause there, feeling your connection to the earth, your friends and family, and the plants and animals that make up your community. Next, bring your k'intu to your head and pause one last time, feeling your connection to the wisdom of spirit. Take a deep breath, bring the bundle to your lips, and blow your hucha into the leaves with one strong exhalation, as if you were blowing out birthday candles. Lift your k'intu up to the sky and offer the heavy energy to

Father Sun, then lower it to the ground and offer it to Mother Earth so she can finish transmuting the heavy energy into clean, pure sámi.

This ceremony can also be done to offer prayers or blessings to the world. Instead of blowing out hucha, you can blow your prayers or blessings into the k'intu and offer it to the appropriate spirit: to Father Sun, Mother Earth, the four directions, the four elements, or anything you choose. Always be clear and focused with your intent, and it will generate powerful results.

Part Two

LLANKAY
THE PATH OF SERVICE

Chapter 4

Sacred Service in Everyday Life

In the little village where I grew up, people worked very hard to grow food, tend their animals, and provide for their families. Later, when my family moved to the city, I saw people working in all kinds of careers. I myself went to work at age eleven, and I quickly learned how to turn my natural gift for chatting up tourists into coins to bring home to my mother.

With all this being the case, you may be surprised to learn that in Quechua, we don't have a word for work! I love telling this to the American guests who come on my tours. "We don't work here," I tell them. "Isn't that good?"

The Spanish word *trabajo* comes from the Latin *trepalium*, which means "to torture" or "to inflict suffering." The French word *travail* comes from the same origin. The English word *labor* comes from the Latin word *laborem*, which refers to toil, exertion, and fatigue. To the Spanish conquerors who attempted to dismantle the Inka culture, work literally meant torture. To this day, many people associate the words *work* and *service* with a burden or even a punishment—for example, if you are convicted of a small crime, you may be sentenced to "community service," as if serving your community is an unpleasant and embarrassing thing!

In the Inka tradition, we don't have this burdensome, punishing idea of work. Indeed, Inka society didn't have a concept of money or wages; instead, people helped out on one another's farms, and they received help in return. Our word for this is *llankay*, which means sacred service. When you carry out llankay, you are giving a hand to Mother Earth, to the Cosmic Mother, to the masters, to the light beings, to the Apus, to Mother Sea, and to all that exists. You are letting their energy express itself through you, for the benefit of all beings. Llankay isn't about the type of service you're doing, but the spirit in which you carry it out. You can engage in sacred service when you're sweeping the floor, programming a computer, cooking a meal, or writing a book, if you do so with the awareness that your actions support your seven sacred relationships.

Every expression of life is in service at all times. The bees are in service to the flowers they pollinate, and the flowers are in service to the bees who drink their nectar. The rain is in service to the crops upon which it falls, and the crops are in service to the people and animals they will feed. Wherever love exists, there is service—and love is everywhere, in all things.

When we embody the spirit of llankay, the work we do in the world is positive and constructive; it builds our character and paves the way to wisdom. We know that we are working not only to make money to provide for our material needs, but to share our light with the world. Every one of us has natural gifts and talents; we are like crystals reflecting different aspects of the sun. Even if the work you do is very humble, it comes from the same divine light and energy as the most rare and specialized work, and it is just as sacred and worthwhile.

In essence, llankay represents your authentic contribution to life that comes from a place of love and light rather than obligation. It is a form of service that brings joy, purpose, and pride rather than suffering or resentment. Perhaps most importantly, it is a form of service that does not discriminate between high and low, valuable or worthless. Every day, Father Sun blesses us with his warmth and light without discrimination. We do not have to be "good" for him to provide that service for us; we do not have to do anything special to deserve it. Every day, our hearts beat and our lungs breathe air, whether the tasks we are engaged in are "important" or humble. The stars in the sky shine on everyone, without asking whether their service is worth it or questioning whether it makes enough of a difference.

In the same way, llankay calls us to serve without asking if we will get anything in return, if the people we serve really deserve it, or if the impact of our service will cross a certain threshold we make up in our minds. Instead, we serve with the goal of sharing our love with all that exists: the people, animals, plants, everything we can see, and everything we cannot see. It doesn't matter if nobody recognizes our service—if we win awards or become famous. We don't need those things to justify sharing our light any more than a mountain needs an award or certificate to bless us with its majesty.

In the modern world, we are obsessed with measuring. How much time are we spending in service? How much are we giving or not giving? How much are we getting paid? We have created a society around measuring, which to me sounds a lot like misery. Measuring, misery—say those words fast and it's hard to tell them apart. Measuring is a path to misery, but serving with an open heart is the path to joy.

Understanding Ayni

The word *ayni* roughly translates to reciprocity. However, it does not simply refer to a tit-for-tat exchange of material goods or services between neighbors, but an exchange of spiritual energy. Ayni is based on the understanding that the souls and spirits of all people are interconnected, and that everything depends on this connection. When you act with ayni, you are respecting and honoring this sacred connection.

Helping others can give you a deep sense of satisfaction and even jubilation. Just imagine sharing a good meal with friends after helping them pack moving boxes all day, or hearing your neighbor's car engine roar to life after tinkering with it together for many afternoons. Far from depleting you or feeling like a burden, you feel energized by the shared accomplishment, especially if it arrived after hours of hard work. Not only that, but your relationship is permanently strengthened by the bond of shared effort on a project.

In contrast, when you withhold your energy from others, or feel resentful about the help you give them, life becomes miserable, and the sense of pride and celebration drains away. Instead of recognizing that you too are constantly receiving help in both seen and unseen ways, you act like an accountant, tallying up a score that is by definition cherry-picked to suit your own limited perspective. The truth is that everything in the world is interdependent; everything assists everything. We are in harmony with the immense cosmos. There is literally no way to accurately account for all the gifts we have been given, or the gifts we ourselves have given to others.

In addition to spiritual beliefs, there are also several practical reasons why ayni became the defining feature of Andean culture. Some anthropologists believe the harsh climate and challenging terrain made it imperative for people to work together to build shelters and grow food. Others suggest that because South America was likely the last land mass on earth to be settled by human beings, requiring a long and arduous journey across the land bridge between Asia and North America, then a long journey south, the people who arrived there must have had strong social bonds and a spirit of cooperation in order to survive. Still others point out that because the Inka civilization didn't have the same extensive trading networks as comparable civilizations elsewhere, they had to engage in constant reciprocity within their own community. For all of these reasons, the spirit of reciprocity lies at the very heart of Andean culture.

In Peru, we believe that a person is not complete if they are not open to both giving and receiving. Some people are excellent givers; they are like a well that never dries. It makes them happy to give their time, money, and energy; they give because it makes them feel good and they know that it is good for themselves and others.

On the other hand, some people are excellent receivers. They can accept compliments with grace, and accept help and advice from others with sincere gratitude and appreciation. They can also make others feel wealthy and abundant by accepting the things that they share. If you have ever given a ride to a friendly hitchhiker or invited some neighbors over to harvest the fruit from your trees, you know how nice it is to be around people who can receive, not just people who give.

In the modern world, the sacred practices of giving and receiving have gotten terribly mixed up. There are entire shelves of self-help books devoted to people who "give too much." We worry that giving to others makes us weak, codependent, pushovers, or easy marks. Advertisements encourage us to put ourselves first, to seek out luxuries that we consume in private rather than sharing our good fortune with our communities. If we do give to others, we are taught to think of it as charity—a good deed rather than a natural expression of ayni.

At the same time, we shame people who receive too much for being needy, dependent, or freeloaders who are living off the hard work of others. When a friend gives us a gift, we start worrying about what we're going to give them in return to balance the scales before we've even had a chance to enjoy it. We focus on the financial wealth people create, while ignoring other ways of contributing value. Indeed, some of the people we scold for being freeloaders give much more to their communities and to Mother Earth than the people who create a lot of material wealth—yet we only see what they take, and ignore what they give.

With such heavy attitudes toward both giving and receiving, we cut off ayni and insulate ourselves, tending to our own needs while doing all that we can to avoid exchanging energy with others. We forget that just by being born at a certain time, in a certain place, we have already received the wisdom and technological advances of those who came before us, just as we will be contributing our own wisdom to the people who come after us. It's impossible to truly quantify all that we have received, or all that we will give throughout our lifetimes. When you shift your perspective to ayni, you realize that such accounting is meaningless.

We all have a deep spiritual need to both give and receive. When we give, we feel our strength and abundance. We get to delight in the unique skills and talents the Cosmic Mother has given us by sharing them with others. We get to feel the creativity, love, and wisdom of the universe flowing through us as we serve, and we get to see the happiness, relief, and gratitude of the people we are serving.

On the other hand, when we receive, we feel the immense love and tenderness the Cosmic Mother has for us. We remember that we are always held in her embrace, and that we don't need to be able to do everything ourselves, because she has placed us among brothers and sisters here on earth who can help us. We get to experience awe at the creativity, love, and wisdom flowing through our neighbors when they give to us.

With this in mind, llankay doesn't just mean providing service to others, but recognizing and cherishing the many acts of service that others do for you, both directly and indirectly. Indeed, it means doing your part to break down the artificial separations between people and working toward the common good. A bountiful harvest benefits everyone; so do beautiful public parks and nature preserves. A community in which every person is fed, clothed, and housed is safer and happier for everyone than a community in which some people suffer in poverty and deprivation while others have much more than they need, and experience the hucha of guilt and fear that goes along with that.

When you recognize the truth of ayni, practicing llankay becomes easy, and what you previously thought of as work becomes the most beautiful gift you have ever known.

Clearing the Obstacles to Service

Just as many of us have inner obstacles that make it difficult to express munay, or unconditional love, it is also very common to have inner resistance to llankay. Often, these obstacles have to do with our cultural conditioning. For example, maybe you were brought up to believe that only a fool does work without getting paid, that the most important thing is to make as much money as possible, or that if you give too much to your neighbors, they will only take advantage of you.

In modern times, many people have a very limited concept of wealth. We think that being rich means having lots of money, a big house, and the resources to travel anywhere you choose. Yet it's common knowledge that you can have all those things and still be miserable. You might be surrounded by material riches, yet have few real friends, no sense of community, and little in the way of joy, spontaneity, or meaning. Not only that, but if your riches came from work rather than service, you might be carrying hucha about the things you did to make your money— especially if it involved exploiting others or Mother Earth.

In Peru, the concept of money didn't even exist until the Spanish came along. People found their wealth in love, community, the beauty of nature, and the deep meaning of their spiritual practice. The goal of work wasn't to accumulate personal riches, but to ensure that everyone in the community was fed, sheltered, and clothed. Practicing llankay puts us back in touch with an expanded concept of wealth that includes things like friendship, peace of mind, and an open heart.

You probably know at least a few people who embody llankay in their lives. For example, maybe you have a friend who is always helping others, and who has a vast and supportive social network as a result; maybe you know someone who has chosen to work in a humble job assisting disabled children or elderly people whose inner sun is always shining brightly. Notice all the positive effects these people are experiencing as a result of their llankay. Talk to them about what service means to them, and how it has enriched their lives even if they have not become wealthy in the limited financial sense of the word. Noticing the benefits of llankay in the lives of people you love and respect will give you the added energy and motivation you need to remove any obstacles you may be carrying to practicing it yourself.

Another common obstacle to practicing llankay is a sense of insignificance. You might ask yourself, *Why does it matter if I protect the environment when so many people are busy extracting as much as they can from Mother Earth? What difference does my small effort make? Why should I make these sacrifices for my neighbors when they don't always seem to notice or care?*

Overcoming this sense of insignificance requires a shift in worldview. In Inka cosmology, nothing is insignificant because everything is connected. Although you may not see an immediate result from your service, that doesn't mean that somewhere in the universe, your service hasn't had an effect in a way you cannot perceive. It's also important to remember the role of hucha and sámi. When your work is dominated by gaining money and riches at the expense of other people and of Mother Earth, you will generate hucha. However, when you live your life in the spirit of service, you generate the light energy of sámi.

Service and Gratitude

Think of a time when someone you know did you a big favor—for example, the neighbor who drove hours to pick you up after your car broke down in a rural place. Chances are, you felt a warm sense of gratitude toward that person long after the incident. Maybe you found yourself becoming very eager to serve that person in some way—by shoveling the snow out of their driveway all winter, or feeding their cat while they were out of town. Even though you might not enjoy shoveling snow or taking care of pets under ordinary circumstances,

I'm going to guess that you carried out these acts of service with eagerness, warmth, appreciation, and maybe even joy.

What happened? Your gratitude for your neighbor transformed what would otherwise be considered work into llankay. Instead of feeling resentful or annoyed by all the snow you have to shovel, you feel grateful to have a chance to repay your neighbor's kindness in the spirit of ayni. The warmth in your heart makes these tasks that might otherwise feel like a pointless burden feel like a gift instead.

How can we hold on to this sense of gratitude when we aren't paying back a favor? All it takes is a shift in perspective: the ability to realize that everything is a favor, and that you are constantly being showered with gifts. For example, it is a beautiful gift to have children whose happy faces greet you every morning when you wake up. To be sure, having children is also a lot of work—but when you cook breakfast for your children, you are saying thank you to the cosmos for sending them to you.

You are also saying thank you to the adults who fed and cared for you when you were a child. Although these experiences may be separated by time and space, the experience of ayni is still there.

It is also a beautiful gift to have strong hands, a clever mind, a charming personality, and other qualities that make it possible to be productive and make a living. Many people do not possess these things. Mother Earth and Father Sun gifted you with these particular qualities so that you could carry out your own unique service in this lifetime. Yet as we are working, we rarely pause to say, "Wow! I am so lucky to have the clever mind that lets me solve these problems" or "I'm so grateful that people find me easy to talk to." Once we realize that it is a gift to be able to do the work that we do, the gratitude we feel is another doorway into llankay.

Finally, we can switch from work to llankay by taking the time to imagine all the creatures, plants, and people our effort will benefit, no matter how humble our tasks may be. For example, when you're sweeping the floor, you can consider the fact that the air quality in your house will be better for everyone to breathe when there isn't too much dust and debris in the air. Not only that, but you will keep the floor in good condition for everyone who lives in that house long after you are gone. If you are selling food at the market, you can reflect on the fact that everyone who eats your food will be nourished and energized; you can take the time to notice the happy expressions on peoples' faces when they smell the delicious aromas of your food or see the dishes beautifully arranged on their plate.

Consciously calling to mind the benefits of your work takes you out of a mindset of isolation and puts you in touch with all the many beings to whom you are connected. When you remember that you are connected to everything, all work is easily transformed into llankay, and everything you do is simply light repaying light in an infinite exchange.

Exercise: Soul Food

With the modern focus on work and money, we sometimes forget that our soul needs beauty in order to thrive. Inviting beauty into your life can help you remember other forms of wealth, which makes it easier to shift from work to llankay.

First, make a practice of simply noticing what feeds your soul. Do you love flower gardens? Colorful tapestries? Delightful fragrances? Beautiful music? Make a point of giving these things your full attention whenever you encounter them. Gather soul nourishment through your eyes by resting them on beautiful sights, through your ears by bathing them in beautiful sounds, and through your heart by fostering loving connections with friends.

Notice how happy and contented you feel when you nourish your soul with beauty. Let this inner wealth fuel the service you carry out, knowing that true riches spring from llankay rather than work.

Exercise: Self-Assessment for Service

At least once a year, it's good to sit down and take inventory of the ways you are bringing llankay to your seven sacred relationships, and identify any relationships in which the spirit of service is perhaps being neglected.

In this exercise, I invite you to sit down with a journal and brainstorm the answers to the following questions:

- How am I in service to the divine feminine?
- How am I in service to the divine masculine?
- How am I in service to my family?
- How am I in service to my community?
- How am I in service to healing the past?
- How am I in service to the future?

- How am I in service to my inner sun?
- Am I carrying any hucha in my relationship to service?

Once you have completed your initial assessment, flip it around and ask yourself the following questions:

- How is the divine feminine serving me?
- How is the divine masculine serving me?
- How is my family serving me?
- How is my community serving me?
- How is the past serving me?
- How is the future serving me?
- How am I serving myself?

Asking yourself both sets of questions and reflecting on them sincerely will help you build your awareness of ayni: the law of reciprocity underlying all things.

Remember that just like munay, bringing llankay to your seven sacred relationships is an ongoing practice. Orienting yourself toward sacred service requires a mindset shift that takes some time to establish. But the more you plant the seeds of service in every relationship, the fuller and richer your life will be.

Chapter 5

Service in Sacred Relationships

Many times when I am speaking about llankay with my American friends, they want to know a list of things they can *do* to be of service. They ask me, "What should I do to serve Mother Earth?" or "What should I do to serve my community?" They think that being of service means adding more tasks and to-dos to their already busy lives, or maybe getting a different job or moving to a different place. I always remind them that while specific acts of service are wonderful, the spirit of llankay isn't so much about what to do as how to be.

In the modern world, we are so used to thinking of ourselves as doers that the concept of llankay can be difficult to grasp. We think that service means doing more, so we add more and more tasks and obligations to our days until we burn out. Then we tell ourselves, "I don't have the energy for this llankay thing, it's too demanding." Another common tendency is to place unrealistic demands on our service. We expect ourselves to solve climate change, save everyone from poverty and disease, and heal all the rifts and conflicts in our families and communities, and when we don't get the results we dreamed of, we feel disappointed and disillusioned.

This is why I always remind my American friends that llankay is how to be, not what to do. If you want to practice llankay in your seven sacred relationships, the first step is not to make a list of things you're going to do, but to cultivate your awareness of ayni until you can perceive the reciprocity flowing through all levels of life at all times. When you are eating, can you feel gratitude for the people who grew those vegetables? When you prepare food for others, can you see how this is connected to your own experiences of being fed? Can you truly feel the connection between what you receive and what you give? Sacred service flows from increased awareness, not by imposing tasks and actions from the outside. The more you become aware of ayni, the more you naturally practice llankay, without trying too hard, until a life of service becomes second nature.

Cultivating Communal Consciousness

The Quechua and Aymara word for family is *ayllu*. The word *ayllu* refers to our extended family, but not just the people with whom we share blood. In the ayllu, we are connected to everything: the mountains, the animals, the plants, the stones, the ancestors who have passed, and even to those who are not yet born. All of these beings are part of our ayllu.

You see, in the Andean tradition, we understand that life is never isolated. The Western mind wants to separate everything: this is nature, this is human, this is animal, this is plant. But the ayllu teaches us that all these expressions of life are interconnected and interdependent. When we live in ayllu consciousness, we make decisions not just for ourselves but for all members of our community. Before we take action, we ask: How will this affect the mountains? How will this affect the waters? How will this affect the children seven generations from now?

In Inka civilization, ayllus were the basic units of society. Each ayllu had its territory that included highland areas and lowland areas, so that people could both graze their animals and grow different types of crops. The ayllu took care of its members. If someone was sick or elderly or could not work, the ayllu made sure they had food, shelter, and clothing. When the Spanish conquerors arrived, they couldn't understand this way of organizing society. They didn't understand why people in the ayllu were taking care of each other instead of keeping as much as possible for themselves. They tried to break the ayllu system, but in many parts of Peru ayllu consciousness continues to this day.

In small villages in Peru, people still live in a largely communal way. They don't say "my land," they say "our land," and they do important tasks like planting and harvesting together. They don't make important decisions alone. Instead, they gather the community. Perhaps most important, they include the mountains, the rivers, the condor, the puma, the serpent, and all of Pachamama in their decision making. This is why I always tell my friends: We don't need to invent new ways to live in harmony on earth. We need to remember the ancient wisdom that has sustained our people for thousands of years. In the ayllu, we find our belonging, our responsibility, and our joy as children of Pachamama and Children of the Sun.

One of the central features of life in the ayllu is called *minka.* Minka is when the community comes together to complete a project for the benefit of all. This is a collective form of llankay that brings joy and harmony to the community, all while getting something done. In ancient times—and still today in many communities in Peru—when someone needed to build a house, or when the fields needed to be prepared for planting, or when the harvest time came, the community would gather in minka. Everyone brings their hands, their hearts, their skills, and they contribute to something that will benefit the whole community or one of its members.

But minka is not *only* work! This is very important to understand. In America, work and play are often strictly separated, but in the Andean tradition, these things are not separate at all. Minka is filled with music, food, laughter, and celebration. The family who receives the help provides *chicha*, or corn beer, and food, and there is singing while the work is being done.

Minka is one more example of ayni in action. Today I help you build your house; tomorrow you help me with my harvest. Nobody keeps score because we understand that we are all interdependent. The cosmos works this way too. Father Sun gives light without asking for payment, and Mother Earth gives food without demanding anything in return—but there is always reciprocity flowing through all things.

The beautiful thing about minka is that it strengthens the fabric of community. When we work together, we remember that we belong to each other. We laugh together, solve problems together, and celebrate together; not only that, but we build memories and stories that become part of our community's lore for generations to come. Minka shows us that work doesn't have to be heavy; service doesn't have to be sacrifice. When we come together with our light, with our love, the work becomes a dance of life.

Often, when visitors come to Peru, they feel something special in their hearts. They feel the love, the connection, and the harmony that our traditions offer. And they often ask me, "Jorge, how can I bring this back home? How can I bring these beautiful traditions into my own life, so far from the Andes?"

I tell them this truth: You don't need to live in Peru to embody the essence of these sacred ways. The wisdom of ayllu and minka exists in your heart already, because your heart knows that these are natural ways to live. These are not just Andean traditions; they are human traditions that the modern world has forgotten.

To cultivate ayllu consciousness where you live, start by expanding your understanding of family. Begin to see the trees near your home as relatives. Try speaking to them, and see what happens! The hummingbirds and bees that visit your garden—they are your family too. Greet them as you would your human friends. The mountains or lakes in your region are grandparents with wisdom to share. Likewise, remember that your ancestors are still with you. Ask for their guidance. Tell them about your life. This is the essence of ayllu:

recognizing that your family circle includes those who have passed and those not yet born.

You can also cultivate ayllu consciousness by making decisions that consider the welfare of all beings. Before you buy something, ask: How will this affect Mother Earth? Before you speak, ask: How will these words affect the harmony of my community? This kind of careful consideration is itself an act of service. Your discernment and restraint form the bedrock of llankay just as much as the positive actions you take in the world.

To cultivate minka, allow your actions to spring from your love for your community. Perhaps you can start a neighborhood meetup where neighbors work together to clean up litter at a park, or organize one day a month when friends or relatives help each other with projects, whether that's trimming the hedges or repainting the lines on the neighborhood basketball court. Remember to include music, food, and festivity. The real treasure of minka isn't the list of tasks you get done, but the opportunity to be in a state of celebration and reciprocity with your neighbors.

Sharing Your Gifts

One beautiful way to bring llankay to your sacred relationships is to discover, cultivate, and share your unique gifts. In a traditional ayllu, everyone contributes what they do best. Some are healers, some are weavers, some are farmers; some take care of children, and some tend to the animals. What are your special gifts? Are you a good listener? Can you do carpentry, fix computers, translate foreign languages, or entertain kids? How can you share these gifts without asking, "What will I get in return?"

In the modern world, we often feel ashamed or bashful about our gifts. We say, "I know how to do a few things, but I'm not a real carpenter" or "I can play a few chords on the guitar, but my voice isn't so good." We compare ourselves to the people we see on TV or social media, who can do incredible things; we tell ourselves that we will be ready to share our gifts when we are finally as good as them.

This hesitation comes from hucha: the energy of guilt that doesn't come from love. When we hold back our gifts because we think they aren't good enough, we are allowing heavy energy to block the natural flow of light through us. We are placing the burden of perfection on our shoulders, as if it is somehow our responsibility to be able to solve every problem, amaze every listener, or accomplish any task.

But just think about children who sing, dance, and draw pictures without worrying if they're good enough, or who are eager to help even if they're too little to swing a hammer or carry a heavy load. They don't hold back until they've mastered a skill or until they're big enough to make a real difference; they express the joy of service in the present moment, exactly as they are. This is true llankay, service that flows from love without calculation or comparison. When we reconnect with this childlike quality, we remember that our gifts aren't about impressing others but about letting our inner sun shine through the talents we have been given.

As Children of the Sun, we are each a unique ray of light. No ray is more important than another: each has its own angle, its own quality, its own purpose. When you share your gifts, whatever they may be, you help weave the beautiful cloth of your community. This cloth needs all kinds of threads: thick and thin, bright and subtle, smooth and textured. In Peru, we say that the most beautiful weavings contain all the colors, all the patterns. In the same way, our community needs all the gifts, not just the most spectacular ones. Your light, exactly as it is today, has an important role to play in the grand cosmic weaving.

Service in Sacred Relationships

Now that we've spent some time talking about how to be, let's return to the subject of what to do. What might it look like to bring the spirit of service to your seven sacred relationships? Here are some ideas.

Service to the mother: We serve the mother by living out our gratitude for all the ways we've been nurtured, fed, and supported throughout our lives. In the Andes, we weave beautiful clothing for Mother Earth by planting vegetables and flowers to cover the bare soil; we also serve the mother by planting trees to clean the air, and making beautiful textiles out of the wool she gives us. Knowing that we have been nurtured, we nurture others by speaking to them with warm words and treating them as our own children.

Service to the father: We serve the father by becoming a ray of light for others. This means smiling at others, encouraging them, and giving them strength and courage in times of difficulty—reflecting their own light back at them so they can see it. Service to the father also means bringing the qualities of clarity, warmth, enthusiasm, and transparency to our speech and actions, so that our most humble act of service is infused with divine grace.

Service to the family: We serve our families by treating their needs and interests as equally important as our own, and taking them into consideration in everything we do. When it comes to our blood or adopted families, this often takes the form of caring for children and the elderly, as well as for those who are disabled. It means calling everyone *brother* or *sister* inside your heart and treating them accordingly, even if you never say those words out loud.

Service to the community: We serve our communities by sharing generously of our gifts and talents, whether that means building a house or being a good listener when someone is sad or upset. In this time of disconnection, serving your community can also mean serving as a point of connection: throwing parties and celebrations, hosting ceremonies, and providing opportunities for people to get together.

Service to the past: We serve the past when we use the strength we have gained from a difficult experience to benefit others. For example, maybe you learned how to cook healthy meals on a tiny budget when you were going through a hard time financially, and now you can share that gift to feed others who are struggling. Maybe you once lived through war, and you now bring the wisdom of peace to every interaction you have. When we affirm and celebrate the gifts we received from difficult experiences, we release any hucha we still carry from those experiences, and use that energy to serve others.

Service to the future: We serve the future whenever we consider the needs of future generations when we carry out our daily tasks. When you take good care of your home or car or any other object you possess, you are extending its useful life and increasing the likelihood that many other people in the future will also be able to it. When you plant trees that will someday shade a park or sidewalk, you are likewise serving the future. And when you work to create fair laws and equal rights in your society, you are doing a meaningful service to the children who will grow up with those laws and those rights.

Service to yourself: We practice service to ourselves by tending to our energy—the balance of hucha and sámi that is always flowing through us. We also serve ourselves by integrating difficult experiences, setting boundaries, and nourishing our relationship with the living earth. Our service to ourself is the bedrock of the service we are able to offer to others, so I've devoted the next chapter to this most important type of llankay.

Exercise: Sunflower Practice

Sunflowers always know where the light is. All day long, they turn their faces to follow the sun. In the same way, we can learn to attune ourselves to the light that powers all our acts of service. Several times throughout the day, go outside and stand facing the sun. Root your feet into the earth, and stand tall like a sunflower. Remember that the light coming from Father Sun also shines in you. Each time, notice how the sun's position has changed in the sky, and how its light and intensity have also changed. Imagine you are connected to the sun through a fine and radiant filament. Repeat this practice until you can feel your connection with the sun throughout the day regardless of whether or not you are outdoors. Allow this connection to give you the energy and inspiration you need to make your life an act of service at every level.

Exercise: Expanding Your Circle of Family

In the Andean tradition, we recognize that all beings who drink water—or what my people call the milk of Mother Earth—are our family. This practice helps you experience this truth not just as an intellectual concept but as a lived reality.

First, pour yourself a glass of water, then go sit in a place where you can see a variety of plants, animals, and people. Hold the glass of water in both hands at the level of your heart. Close your eyes, and reflect on how this water connects you to all beings. Say aloud or silently: "This water I hold has cycled through countless beings throughout time. It has been part of oceans, clouds, rivers, plants, animals, and humans. It connects me to all life on earth."

Next, take a small sip of water, letting it linger in your mouth. Feel gratitude for this gift from Mother Earth. Open your eyes and look around you. Notice any plants, trees, animals, insects, or people nearby. Say to each one in your heart: "You who drink the same water as I do, you are my family. We share the milk of Mother Earth."

Take another sip of water. Now close your eyes and visualize each of these things:

- The people you already consider family
- People you know but don't think of as family
- People you find difficult or challenging
- Animals, including pets, domesticated animals, and wild animals

- Plants and trees
- Rivers, lakes, and oceans
- Mountains and stones

As each image appears, greet it with these words: "You who drink the same water as I do, you are my family. We share the milk of Mother Earth."

Extend your practice to include beings you cannot see—the microorganisms in the soil, the creatures in the deep ocean, even those who lived long ago or will live in the future.

The next time you're out in the world and find yourself in a challenging interaction with another person, pause and remember: "This is my family drinking the same water as I do." Notice how your behavior naturally shifts when you view others as family rather than strangers or adversaries. As this practice becomes second nature, you'll find yourself spontaneously recognizing family everywhere you go.

Chapter 6

Self-Care as Sacred Service

In the steep mountainside villages of the Andes, the llama has long been a symbol of service. These humble creatures have served Andean peoples for thousands of years in many different ways. They carry bundles of food, medicine, and other supplies along narrow and winding mountain paths. Their dung fertilizes the soil in the gardens, their meat provides sustenance, and their wool keeps people warm.

Yet despite all these many demands, you won't see a llama hurrying, putting up with mistreatment, or working itself to exhaustion. Llamas are famous for walking at a relaxed pace of one and half to two miles per hour, which is slower than some speed-obsessed humans. Like humans, llamas don't like to carry more than 20 to 25 percent of their body weight. Indeed, if a load is too heavy, a llama will simply kneel and refuse to move until the burden is adjusted. Llamas also insist on frequent breaks to rest their bodies, and rarely walk more than nine miles in one day—often less.

The llama's wisdom reminds us that sacred service is *not* the same thing as martyrdom or self-sacrifice. Just as the llama knows when to walk and when to rest, we too must find balance in our service, honoring our limits while still contributing our gifts. We cannot give to others if we do not also give to ourselves. This is a basic principle, yet it is so easy to forget. The way we carry our own burdens determines our ability to carry the burdens of others; we cannot provide food or fertilizer if we ourselves are not well fed. We cannot keep others warm if we do not use warm words with ourselves, or make beauty for others if we do not cultivate beauty in our own lives.

Often, we struggle to serve ourselves because we were taught that it is selfish, or that it is shameful to tend to our own needs when there are so many people whose needs are greater than our own. Other times, we have difficulty serving ourselves because we are consumed by our own thoughts and emotions and don't know how to balance them. The hucha we carry feels overwhelming, and we forget that we can always release it using ceremony and other tools. We also forget that we can use spiritual practices to cultivate the sámi that fills our being with light.

When we serve other people, we only see their outsides; but when we serve ourselves, we have to contend with our insides—and for many of us, this is much harder! When we slow down enough to practice llankay toward ourselves, we often have to face emotions like fear and guilt that we would prefer not to feel. Yet it is only by working with these heavy energies that we can release them back to Mother Earth where they belong. Sacred self-care often means courageously looking at the aspects of ourselves we would prefer to keep hidden, trusting that we are capable of the most powerful transformations when we tap into the light of our inner sun.

Dancing with Opposites

The Quechua word *tinkuy* means "to encounter" and refers to the coming together of two seemingly distinct or even opposing energies to create something new: for example, light reflecting on water or masculine energy meeting feminine energy. The Inka believed that instances of tinkuy were charged with power, and they put a great deal of effort into seeking out such instances in nature, or even creating new ones—for example, by placing stones or channels of water where they would be illuminated on a solstice or form a cross when the Milky Way crossed the line of an eclipse.

When we witness a moment of tinkuy, we feel powerful emotions of awe, reverence, and humility in the face of the vastness of the cosmos. We remember that there is something out there that is much bigger than ourselves, and that whatever service we carry out during our time here on earth is just one small piece of a much bigger whole. We marvel at the way the stars and planets align, following their trajectories perfectly with no help or interference from us. Most important, we remember that the universe is working through us—our service isn't something we create, but a gift we express. Remembering these things replenishes the spirit and gives us much-needed perspective on our lives.

Experiences of tinkuy aren't limited to stunning natural events like solar eclipses or meteor showers; tinkuy is also present in human relationships. We can have powerful encounters with other people, including total strangers, when we sing, dance, or do satisfying work together. In such moments, the illusion of separation falls away, and we realize that these people who may seem so different from us on the surface all share the same inner sun. Looking into a baby's eyes, or into the eyes of a very old person, can also be a moment of tinkuy, as you see a timeless energy reflected in these seemingly opposite stages of life.

In Andean spirituality, we believe that nothing is ever truly in opposition; everything is always part of the whole. Tinkuy is the understanding that life is a dance, and to dance, we need a partner. We have partners in every aspect of life, in the visible world and the invisible world. When you feel fear, it means that courage is also there; when you feel guilt, it means that innocence is also present. When a part of you dies, another part is simultaneously coming to life. When you feel burned out and overwhelmed, it means that replenishment is also available—you just need to stop seeing yourself as separate, and reconnect to the whole.

When you are living from your inner sun, you are always in your center—and when you are in your center, you have 360 degrees of possibilities, and you can dance with the cosmos. This is a position of strength from which you can easily balance heavy energies and light energies as they arise, dissolving seeming oppositions and disharmonies within your own being.

However, when you are not in your center, you get pulled to the periphery. You are still dancing—the only thing is, now something at the periphery is directing the dance. Maybe it's fear, maybe it's pride, maybe it's regret. When you are dancing at the periphery, the outside world controls you, the situations control you, and your thinking mind with its ideas about what you should be controls you. But when you are in your center, those same situations can exist without pulling you in.

The key to sacred self-care is to stay in your center at all times. This means consciously remembering that your life is supported by the service of the cosmos, and learning to stay within this cosmic perspective instead of getting pulled into the superficial details of your life. Knowing that you are a sacred part of this vast universe, you can also make a practice of using warm words with yourself at all times. Just think about it: out of all possible manifestations of life, the Cosmic Mother and Father entrusted you to yourself. You are already sacred; you possess the same light as everything you consider beautiful and precious. You deserve to speak to yourself just as tenderly as the Comic Mother speaks to you.

Another way to stay in your center is to maintain awareness of the stories your mind is telling you. We all tell ourselves stories—that's one of the defining features of being human. But all too often, we forget that we are the ones telling the stories, and we start to see every one of them as true. When you consider the fact that the thinking mind has a tendency to generate negative and fearful thoughts, this can quickly turn into a big problem, pulling us out of our center and attaching us to whatever drama we've created in our mind.

Staying in your inner sun means knowing how to dissolve those stories by holding them up to the light. For example, if you have a story that you are worthless, ask yourself, "Why do I feel that way? Where did this story come from? What is the purpose of this story in my life?" Look at this story with all the clarity, transparency, warmth, and enthusiasm of Father Sun, and notice if it begins to feel less true and solid than it did before. Heavy energy thrives on vagueness, obscurity, and lack of investigation, but when we bring it fully into the light, it tends to dissolve on its own.

When you find yourself being pulled to the periphery of your being by fear, judgment, or by a story that carries heavy energy, all you have to do is turn toward the light of your inner sun. Witness the beautiful tinkuy between the warmth and light of your inner sun and the heaviness of that energy, and welcome the ensuing transformation into your heart.

Setting Sacred Boundaries

Often, we confuse llankay with giving up our boundaries. A neighbor asks for a favor; a family member wants to come over late at night; the community center needs a volunteer for the food drive on the weekend. You want to be of service, so you don't say no. Before you know it, you're burned out. You want to hide from people in case they ask you for something you're already too tired to give. As if that wasn't bad enough, you feel guilty, even though you're doing so much. You start generating hucha from all that guilt, and it becomes a heavy burden on your body, mind, and heart.

Maybe you also take on hucha from the problems of the world. You see all the terrible things in the news—the environmental destruction, the wars, the poverty—and you feel like it's your personal responsibility to make everything right. You don't have a clear sense of what's really yours, and so you take on everything, feeling guilty about things that were set in motion long before you were born.

Any time you feel isolated, overwhelmed, and as if you are carrying the weight of the world on your shoulders, it means you have slipped out of llankay and entered into a state of martyrdom or unhealthy self-sacrifice. When you serve with the spirit of llankay, you never feel alone because you know that you are working in concert with all that exists. You never carry the whole world on your shoulders, because you can see that you are intimately connected to all beings, who are likewise carrying the world for you. Just as your love is an aspect of divine love, and your wisdom is an aspect of the divine wisdom that permeates the cosmos, your service is also an aspect of the divine service that is always present.

With this in mind, practicing llankay means both recognizing your essential state of connection to all beings *and* saying no to heavy energy that isn't yours to take on. If you are too physically, mentally, or emotionally exhausted to carry out a certain task or accept a certain responsibility, it's okay to be like the llama: to pause, take a rest, and adjust or even jettison anything that is too heavy for you to carry.

Saying no to a certain task or obligation doesn't mean you are shirking your sacred service; rather, it means you are recognizing what your body, mind, and spirit need to stay in balance, so you can be of service in the long term. Remember, the essence of life is to bring harmony to all seven of your sacred relationships, including your relationship with yourself. Sacrificing this essential relationship in the name of a different relationship isn't good for anyone.

When done properly, llankay gives us energy rather than depleting us; it strengthens our connections rather than fraying them; and it gives us purpose rather than overwhelming us with impossible demands. Once you recognize that you too are worthy of receiving care and service, you can be like the llama: going at a relaxed pace, resting frequently, and asserting your boundaries when the load is too heavy for you to bear.

Working with Different Energies

In Andean spirituality, we recognize many different kinds of energy. You've already learned about hucha and sámi. Now I would like to briefly talk about two more types of energy: *kawsay* and *camay*. Kawsay is the organic vitality of living beings such as animals and flowers: the energy that makes grass grow and birds hatch out of their eggs. In contrast, camay refers to inorganic vitality: the cosmic energy found in stones and crystals, as well as the shells, bones, and feathers left behind by various living beings after their kawsay has departed from their bodies.

In other words, we believe that just because a stone, mountain, or star isn't alive the same way a condor or puma is alive, they nevertheless contain and transmit vital energy.

In fact, just like the ancient Egyptians, the Inka believed that human remains continue to exude camay long after the kawsay has left the body; this is why both cultures practiced mummification. To this day, spiritual practitioners throughout Peru keep ancestral skulls and other relics on their altars: these objects continue to transmit cosmic vitality even after their organic life has ended.

In Quechua, the verb *camay* means "to animate" or "to infuse with life." Running water such as rivers and streams were seen as a powerful force of camay, giving life to plants. Noticing the power of water to bring life and abundance to the earth, the Inkas incorporated the pouring of water into their rituals and ceremonies, believing it could awaken sentience in stones, carvings, and other objects. For this reason, many Inka sacred sites are located near running water, which charges the nearby outcroppings, caves, and mountains with camay.

The Inkas also believed that stars and other celestial bodies had the power of camay. For example, llamas were believed to get their cosmic vitality from the llama-shaped constellation in the sky; and eclipses and other phenomena were believed to give camay to the sacred sites with which they were aligned.

When we understand the principle of camay, we can seek out the sources of cosmic vitality in our own lives and use them to replenish ourselves. What animates your spirit and gives you energy? What is the magical wellspring from which your existence flows? How can you work with this source of camay to balance your energy and expand your capacity to serve?

One of my favorite ways to balance my energy is by working with crystals and stones. Peru is rich in naturally occurring crystals such as the Peruvian opal, black jade, and pink opal. Because they are a powerful source of camay, stones, minerals, and crystals play an important role in Andean spiritual practices. Indeed, legend has it that the Inka creation god Wiraqocha made the first people out of stone, before creating the sun, stars, and moon.

I like to gather stones that call to me when I visit the mountains. Mountains are silent watchers and protectors; in Peru, we consider them to be multidimensional beings, inhabiting both the present-day world and the world of the divine simultaneously. When I pick up a stone from a mountaintop, I introduce myself by blowing on it; however, I'm not blowing air, but light from my heart. In return, the stone will speak to me, sharing its camay with me. In my own practice, I use black stones like tektite to pull out heavy energies, and clear crystals for cleansing. Because they come from the Apus, stones help us bridge our inner and outer worlds.

Another wonderful way to work with camay is to visit a body of water that is sacred to you, such as a stream, lake, or Mama Qocha, the ocean. In Peru, people often go on pilgrimage to the Lagunas de las Huaringas, a set of fourteen sacred lagoons in the Huamaní mountain range. People believe that bathing in the beautiful, cold waters of las Huaringas brings spiritual purification, healing, and an increase in vitality, all of which gives them the energy they need to carry out their llankay in everyday life.

But you don't need to live near a famous pilgrimage site to revitalize yourself with camay. Simply find a place in nature where you can sit quietly and observe a source of organic vitality, whether it's a mountain, a waterfall, or the stars in the sky. This can be all the reminder you need that the energy in your body is a gift from the universe, and that your llankay is the gift you give back to the universe that created you. With this awareness, it becomes easy to care for yourself without taking on too much or giving too little, knowing that you are a Child of the Sun.

Exercise: Walking with Pachamama

One of the best ways to practice self-care is to consciously cultivate your connection to Pachamama. You don't need special training or initiations to connect to Pachamama—you are already connected to her, and the umbilical cord was never cut. In this exercise, I invite you to release anything that doesn't come from love into Mother Earth, and receive her nourishment in return.

First, prepare a small offering such as flower petals, coca leaves, spring water, or herbs from your local environment.

Next, go to a natural space such as a forest, park, or lake. Choose a grassy or sandy spot where you can stand, sit, and lie down comfortably. Place your offering on the earth. As you do so, express your thanks for all the gifts Mother Earth has given you: from the beautiful trees and flowers in your environment, to the air you breathe, to the water you drink, to the incredible body that lets you move around and experience life.

Next, take off your shoes and socks. Stand on the earth, feeling the connection through your feet. Pay attention to how the energy in your body changes when you touch the ground directly, instead of through shoes or sandals.

Now lie down on the earth. Allow the feeling of connection to spread through your whole body.

Remember the unbroken umbilical cord that ties you to Pachamama every day of your life. Imagine yourself releasing any heavy energy you've been carrying into the earth. Use this connection to let go of guilt, rejections, old beliefs that don't serve you, and any energy that doesn't come from love. Feel Mother Earth receiving this energy; you might even visualize her composting it into rich, fertile soil.

When you feel complete, sit up slowly and look around. Notice how all the beautiful plants in your environment grew out of the earth. Remember that the heavy energy, which might seem bad or negative, is just food for Mother Earth to create these beautiful things.

Exercise: Journal Practice for Release

Sometimes, our bodies feel heavy or even become ill because we have not fully released the hucha from our minds. In this exercise, I invite you to cleanse your emotional body through journaling, which will in turn affect how you feel on the physical plane.

First, get a notebook or journal and a pen, and find a quiet space to sit. Now start writing in the third person. For example, instead of writing, "I woke up feeling sad and my head hurts," write, "He woke up feeling sad and his head hurts." This helps creates a healthy distance between you and your heavy emotions. Allow yourself to be completely honest. Write quickly, without censoring yourself. Describe what's going on in your mental, physical, and emotional body, and name what you need to release. Keep going for at least fifteen minutes, then stop when you feel complete.

Repeat this practice every day for twenty to thirty days. Notice how the heavy energies dissolve and the issues become lighter when you allow yourself to write them down in detail. Notice too if writing about these energies in the third person gives you a new perspective on old stories, or even helps you laugh about them.

At the end of thirty days, you can feed your journal pages to a fire—or what we call Mama Nina in Quechua. If you have taken on too much and fallen out of balance, it can be extremely cathartic to write it all down and let Mama Nina transform the pages before your eyes—reminding you that you are not your story, but a part of nature, just like her.

Part Three

YACHAY
THE PATH OF WISDOM

Chapter 7

The Wisdom of the Three Worlds

I once asked some Andean elders, "What is the most important thing for a chakaruna to learn? Some people say it's about developing the gift to see—to see the past, to see the future."

But the elders replied, "No, it's not about that. It's not about becoming something, a powerful healer, magician, or fortune teller. No, it's not about that."

"Okay," I said. "What about traveling across the world, visiting power places, and drinking in the energy from those power places?"

"Oh no," they assured me. "Being a chakaruna is not about that."

"Okay," I said. "So it's not about going places, it's not about gaining special powers, and it's not about seeing the past or predicting the future. Then what does it mean to be a chakaruna?"

The elders replied, "Becoming a chakaruna means learning to see that there is only one life. When you can do that, you are truly wise."

The wisdom to which the elders were referring is called yachay, or divine wisdom, as opposed to the formal knowledge you get from going to school and reading books. Yachay is inseparable from munay and llankay. Love and service build our wisdom, but we can also use wisdom to discern how best to be of service, and how to remove any barriers we have to love.

Most of the time, our thoughts and opinions spring only from the thinking mind. Unfortunately, the thinking mind is also where the ego lives—which means that most of our thoughts and opinions come from the ego. Instead, we must learn to think, feel, and experience life from the perspective of our inner sun. When we do this, we can see all of life through the lens of yachay, and make decisions based on love that take our seven sacred relationships into account, instead of decisions motivated by fear that we later regret.

How can you really know if you are growing spiritually? Your ego-based mind might say, "You're practically a master! You've done so many initiations, and have such great insights into the past and future." But if you look at this question through the eyes of wisdom, you see that spiritual growth can only be measured by the harmony you have in your seven sacred relationships. You are only a master when you realize the oneness of life.

Bridging the Worlds

In Inka cosmology, there are three realms which all humans inhabit at all times: *Ukhu Pacha*, *Kay Pacha*, and *Hanan Pacha*. Each of these three realms has its own wisdom to offer. The word *pacha* means "world," "place," or "space," yet these three worlds aren't considered to be separate from each other. Instead, they exist simultaneously, and we can access them freely; indeed, they are a part of us. The three realms are an important concept, so let's take a look at each one in more detail.

Ukhu Pacha is sometimes called the lower world or the underworld, although I prefer to think of it as the *inner* world. Western psychotherapists might refer to this as the realm of the subconscious: the place where all our memories and experiences are stored and processed, or in some cases, suppressed and unprocessed.

Ukhu Pacha is the home of Amaru, the sacred two-headed serpent who represents wisdom. Amaru is a master of transformation, gifted with the ability to shed his skin. He is not afraid of the inner world, but knows that contemplation and reflection hold the key to awakening. We just need the courage to enter the places we've unconsciously declared off-limits.

So often, our wisdom is hidden in the darkness. Just as many of us are afraid of snakes, we are likewise afraid of our own inner knowing—afraid that our lives will get turned upside down if we pay attention to what we know deep inside. For example, maybe you know you need to leave some job or lifestyle that isn't right for you, but you ignore this wisdom out of fear. The wisdom is there, but you're afraid that you'll fail, that you won't have enough, or that people will judge you—and so you bury it.

Amaru calls us to uncover this inner world that we have buried, and let go of the heavy energies which block us from yachay. Often, the fears we have spring from the pain we still carry from the past: the anger, impotence, guilt, shame, and other forms of hucha we developed as a result of receiving judgments and criticisms from other people or from ourselves. Bringing these heavy energies into the light helps them transform, liberating us to make the changes we need in our lives.

Amaru goes deep into our inner world to cleanse us. He goes to our dark, scared, and forgotten places to help us discover and accept any hucha we are carrying so we can release it and recognize our true nature as Children of the Sun. It is only once we release our hucha that we can unlock the wisdom we gained from our past experiences. When the serpent helps us to eliminate our heavy energy with love and gratitude, we can peel off the old skin that has become too tight and let ourselves breathe freely. This brings us closer to our true essence, our inner sun. With help from Amaru, we radiate the transparent light of yachay, our inner wisdom no longer suppressed and ignored.

Kay Pacha is often referred to as the middle world. It is our everyday world, the here and now—the world in which we live and carry out our daily tasks. Some people refer to Kay Pacha as the external world, because it is where we create the face and personality we show to other people, which may be very different from the self we experience in the inner world of Ukhu Pacha.

Navigating Kay Pacha also takes wisdom. After all, this is the world in which we are called to bring our contributions, talents, and gifts forward for the evolution of life. As we go about our days, we are constantly challenged to make wise decisions and solve moral dilemmas, which don't always have obvious answers. We experience conflict with our parents, our children, or in other relationships, and need wisdom to find a kind, heartfelt, and compassionate way through them.

In Inka mythology, Kay Pacha is associated with the puma. The sacred qualities of the puma include humility, flexibility, and adaptability. She does what she needs to do without calling attention to herself. Indeed, many times, people don't even realize she was there until they find her paw prints! She hunts with stealth and in silence, without ego. In the Andes, we think of the puma as being flexible and adaptable because she can walk equally well in the highlands as the lowlands.

Connecting to the spirit of the puma gives us the courage we need to carry out our sacred tasks on the earthly realm and to make decisions that serve our best and highest good. Puma energy keeps us focused in this world, instead of drifting off into fantasies and becoming ungrounded. She reminds us that the point of spiritual practice isn't to escape our lives, but to live more skillfully; not to gain special powers, but to master the earthly tasks we were put here to do.

The puma is also the stalker of the mind, the witness to our experiences and internal conversations. She observes our thoughts and attitudes and helps us see if our feelings come from love or are brought on by fear. It is the puma's great control, combined with her courage, that helps us grow in the wisdom we need to navigate the everyday world.

Hanan Pacha is known as the upper or celestial world. It's the realm of light and light beings, including ascended masters and spiritual teachers, but it is also the home of the divine self that lives inside each one of us. It is here that we connect to a timeless wisdom much greater than ourselves: the wisdom of Father Sun, Mother Earth, the Apus, and all celestial beings.

Hanan Pacha is associated with the condor, who has the power to fly vast distances and observe all that happens in Kay Pacha from a higher vantage point. The condor gives us the wisdom of perspective. Often, we get so caught up in the dramas unfolding in Kay Pacha that we forget that our essential nature is divine, eternal, and luminous. We allow temporary setbacks to obscure our inner sun, or we focus on superficial conflicts while losing sight of the essential harmony of all things. It takes wisdom to pause, reflect, and remember that these events and their outcomes are quite small in the grand scheme of things.

The condor also teaches us the wisdom of traveling light by unburdening ourselves of anything that doesn't serve our highest good. When the condor sets his sights on a sacred destination, he releases any hucha that might be holding him back from getting there. He knows the only way he can truly be free to fly as high as he wants is by eliminating any extra weight that might drag him down.

Yet just as the condor teaches us to fly, he also teaches us the importance of coming back down to earth for a secure landing. Spiritual practice isn't about pulling up stakes in Kay Pacha and making a new home for yourself in some celestial realm far away, but bridging these worlds in a safe, grounded, and effective manner. We must always complement our cosmic flight with a predictable landing, just as the condor returns to his nest. True yachay consists of integrating the three worlds, not escaping or suppressing any one of them.

The serpent, the puma, and the condor remind us that the three worlds are all connected. The wisdom of your subconscious affects the actions you carry out in the middle world; your responsibility and maturity in the middle world pave the way for you to receive wisdom from the upper world; and the wisdom you receive from the upper world gives you the clarity you need to tend to your middle and lower worlds in a skillful way. The three Pachas are not separate, but interwoven in a state of constant exchange. It is by embracing all three that we become truly wise.

Clearing the Obstacles to Wisdom

Just as we sometimes struggle to practice munay and llankay, we sometimes struggle to distinguish true yachay from the thoughts, opinions, and judgments that come from our ego. We might tell ourselves that we are practicing wisdom when we are really just living out the habits and conditioning with which we were raised; we might tell ourselves we are being wise, when we are really being selfish or fearful. Yet with practice, you can develop a felt sense of when you are coming from your thinking mind as opposed to the yachay of your inner sun.

Many of us weren't raised with the belief that we could cultivate inner wisdom. We think that wisdom belongs to a guru or spiritual teacher—it is something that an outside figure has to hand down to us, not something that arises naturally from the depths of our own being. Yet when you feel a strong inner knowing, it is unmistakable. The knowledge seems to originate in your heart instead of from your head. Indeed, your mind gets very quiet, with the ordinary chatter fading away, when you tap into the energy of yachay. But in order to do this, you need to give up the belief that wisdom belongs only to "special" people who have advanced training or initiations.

Another common obstacle to yachay is worry. Worry is a trickster with a million disguises. Sometimes, worry disguises itself as responsibility, maturity, or good judgment; other times, we tell ourselves that worry is a form of love for ourselves and others. We say things like, "I wouldn't be a good mom if I didn't worry so much about my kids" or "If I wasn't so worried about climate change, I wouldn't bother planting trees or donating to environmental causes." Worry masquerades as virtue, a necessary motivator for us to do the right thing.

Yet worry is nothing more than fear by another name. When we constantly worry, we create fear frequencies that cloud our inner sun, making it difficult to access yachay. This is because worry is based in the mind; worries are made of thoughts, which keep us isolated in our own narrow perspective and cause us to forget the cosmic perspective. For example, maybe you worry that you won't get the job you applied for—and indeed, you may not get it. But instead, you end up in a job that's much better suited to your talents than the one you originally applied for. If you listen to your worries, not getting the first job was a disaster; yet all along, the wisdom of the universe was working through you to lead you onto a better path.

As another example, many people who visit Peru worry that they will not have time to see all the sacred sites and architectural marvels, and so they rush from place to place, never fully taking anything in. Yet if you are guided by yachay, you know that you are always in the right place at the right time. Instead of rushing to see everything on your list, you can connect fully to the energy of the place you happen to be, and to the people who happen to be there with you. Visitors who are guided by yachay always have a much deeper experience than those who are led by worry.

Other obstacles to yachay include being cut off from your body, from your emotions, and from Pachamama. When you are in a state of disconnection, your being is inherently stressed, and it is very difficult to make wise decisions from this state. Not only that, but if you limit yourself to the wisdom of your thinking mind, you're missing out on the various kinds of wisdom that are constantly being communicated to you in nonverbal ways. I will say more about tapping into these kinds of wisdom in the next chapter.

The Eleven Eyes of Wisdom

When you see life through the eyes of fear, worry, and judgment, yachay becomes clouded and hard to access. When it comes time to make an important decision, all you can think about is all the bad things that might happen. You think, *I had better look out for myself, even if it means other people get a bad deal.* You make your decision out of fear, and then you have to live with the consequences. Later, you ask yourself, "Why did I do that? I could have chosen a more harmonious path. What was I thinking? Where was my yachay?"

Cultivating yachay means seeing life through the eyes of love. In the Inka tradition, we believe we have eleven eyes. These eyes allow us to perceive all three pachas and navigate smoothly between them, drawing in the wisdom of each one. The eleven eyes include the following:

- The seven chakras, or sacred energy centers, located at the base of the spine, the lower abdomen, the solar plexus, the heart, the throat, the eyebrows, and the top of the head.
- The two physical eyes
- One eye above the crown chakra (top of the head)
- One eye below the root chakra (base of the spine)

Just as we clean the windows in our house so they stay clear and bright, we must also clean these spiritual eyes so we can receive all the light that is constantly streaming our way. Sometimes when you move into a new house, all the rooms are spotless and shining. But after some years, you think, "Wow, this house isn't as nice as I thought it was—I need to paint the walls and get a new rug." But what really happened? You forgot to wash the windows, and now the sunlight can't get in!

The same thing happens with our perception. Each one of our spiritual eyes is there to let the light in, but just like windows, they can get dusty. We get stressed or busy, we get hooked by gossip or heavy energy, we stop taking care of our bodies, and suddenly these beautiful windows are no longer letting in so much light. When this happens, we need to refresh and restore our spiritual eyes so that we can once again see the world through the light of wisdom.

With the physical eyes alone, we see just a little bit. But when we cleanse and open all eleven eyes, we can see the full picture: how all life is interconnected. We begin to understand that there is only one life, and everything exists in reciprocal service to each other. When we open the eyes of the spirit, we connect with the wisdom of the cosmos, we perceive refined energies, we recognize the light and love in all beings, and we understand our role in service to all life.

The path of wisdom calls us to look beyond our own individual experience—to recognize that our body does not end at the tips of our fingers and toes, but extends to include the whole earth and everything on it. We cannot be truly healthy if people in our community are sick; we cannot be truly wealthy if people in our community are poor; and we cannot be truly happy if people in our community are suffering. And of course, the same thing is true not only of our human neighbors, but of plants, animals, water, and all of Pachamama.

When we are children, we think all the time about what we want, what's fair and unfair, and how to get more for ourselves. But as we grow in yachay, we deeply understand the interconnections between all beings. This understanding makes us generous, selfless, compassionate, and kind—the core qualities of a chakaruna.

Exercise: Cleansing Your Spiritual Eyes

One way to cleanse your spiritual eyes is by using the "triangle of light."

First, go outside at either sunrise or sunset—in other words, a time when the sun is *not* at its peak intensity, but is still easy to see in the sky. Next, stack your hands so they form a triangle with a tiny hole at the center between the base of your thumbs. This hole should be just big enough to let in a pinprick of light when you hold your hands up to the sun.

Stand facing the sun, and lift your hands so that pinprick of light comes through. Notice how the light splits into different colors. Feel the qualities of each color. Let yourself experience the living light.

Now feel this light running through your body like water, cleansing and purifying each of your eleven eyes one at a time. Bring your attention to each eye in turn, noticing how the light polishes it and washes away any stagnant energy.

Once you have cleansed all eleven eyes, bring your hands to your heart and close your eyes. Notice any images that appear. Feel how the light stays with you, a living presence in your body and spirit, even once the practice is done.

Remember: This light is love. This light is wisdom. This light is life. Use it to cleanse your spiritual eyes whenever you need clarity; the light is always there for you if you let it in.

Exercise: Bridging the Three Worlds

Recall that in Inka cosmology, the three worlds are not separate but richly interwoven. In this exercise, I invite you to summon the wisdom of each world and its animal spirit, linking them together through your body and mind.

First, find a quiet space where you won't be disturbed. If possible, do this practice outdoors where you can connect directly with Mother Earth and Father Sun. Take three deep breaths to center yourself.

Now sit on the ground and close your eyes. Take a moment to connect to your inner self. Visualize the wise serpent, Amaru, coming to you from the depths of Ukhu Pacha. Say: "I am a Child of the Sun rooted in Ukhu Pacha. I embrace all the experiences of my past with courage and love. Like the serpent, I shed old beliefs and identities that no longer serve me."

Pause for a few breaths, and listen for any messages Amaru has to share from your inner world. These messages might come in the form of thoughts, images, intuitions, or physical sensations.

Next, open your eyes and stand up. Imagine a puma standing by your side with grace and confidence, its head held high. Say: "I am a Child of the Sun living in Kay Pacha. I bring my gifts, talents, and contributions forward for the evolution of life. Like the puma, I walk with flexibility and courage."

Pause for a few breaths, and listen for any messages the puma has to share from your life in Kay Pacha.

Now extend your arms out to your sides like the wings of the condor. Imagine yourself flying high above the earth, seeing the bigger picture of your life, gaining perspective and wisdom. Say: "I open myself to the divine wisdom of Hanan Pacha. I rise like the condor to see the greater panorama of life. I release whatever is holding me back from flying high and free."

Pause for a third and final time, and listen for any messages the condor has to share from the spiritual realm.

Finally, bring your hands together in front of your heart, forming a triangle with your thumbs and index fingers. Feel the wisdom of all three worlds flowing through your mind, body, and spirit. Say: "I bring the wisdom of the serpent, the courage of the puma, and the perspective of the condor into my daily life for the benefit of all beings."

Repeat this practice anytime you feel cut off from an aspect of your sacred wisdom.

Chapter 8

Wisdom Beyond the Mind

In the modern, industrialized world, we tend to associate wisdom with the thinking mind. Indeed, in our pursuit of this type of wisdom, we may stay up late studying, drinking pots of coffee to override our body's exhaustion so we can cram more information into our brains, or skimming piles of articles in rapid succession without truly absorbing what we are reading. We spend so much time consuming media in the form of videos, podcasts, and online articles that we literally forget where we are—on a living, breathing planet, in a living, breathing body.

In our quest to acquire more facts and master more skills, we fall out of balance.

As I explained in the previous chapter, Inka spirituality emphasizes the ability to engage with life on multiple levels: not only with the intellect, but with our bodies, emotions, and spirits. When all these different modes of perception come into balance, that's when we become truly wise; that's when we harness the energy of yachay.

Our body is a powerful tool that allows us to feel energy. When we are attuned to our bodies, we can more easily perceive information about whether a certain person, place, or thing is healthy or unhealthy for us. For example, if you are cut off from your body's wisdom, you may ignore the clenching in your stomach that tells you a certain person is untrustworthy or that a situation is dangerous, but you may be equally likely to ignore signs that a person or situation is loving and safe.

Similarly, when you are cut off from the wisdom of your body, you may allow stress to build up in your system, either though overwork or overthinking. You may attempt to manage this stress by drinking, abusing drugs, endlessly scrolling the internet, or otherwise numbing the sensations in your body instead of listening to them. This creates a vicious cycle, in which you become more and more stressed, and more and more cut off.

All the cells in our body are in service to our life—every single one. Every hair on your head, every drop of blood in your veins, every eyelash is in service to your existence here on earth. The intelligence of the universe runs through your body at every level. Once you realize this, it becomes impossible to hate your body or to engage in activities that diminish your health. Instead, you become curious about the wisdom your body has to share: the way it seems to know things before your mind does, and the way it is constantly picking up subtle information from your environment that your mind can't always explain.

Some people say, "Oh, I hate my belly, I hate my big feet." If you are not happy with your belly, how do you think you would live without all the work your belly does? Your stomach receives and processes the food you need to live. Your feet let you stand, walk, and run. These things have been in service to you every day of your life, and have wisdom you cannot begin to comprehend. How do your feet know how to balance with every step, even on rugged terrain? How does your stomach know how to break down all kinds of food, even when you are traveling in an unfamiliar place? You couldn't make those calculations with your conscious mind, but your body has the wisdom to do it automatically.

Loving your body doesn't just mean being at peace with your physical appearance—it means feeling curiosity, wonder, and gratitude for the many complex functions your body carries out, and doing your best to support it in those functions instead of making its job harder. Your body lets you feel the warm and bright sensations of munay, it helps you carry out the tasks that are central to your expression of llankay, and it also helps you grow in yachay when you pay attention to the subtlety of its signals.

In the Inka tradition, we view the body as both a physical vessel *and* an energetic instrument—a part of ourselves that can sense and transmit energy while also requiring care and appreciation. The body is yet another bridge between the earthly and the divine. After all, we couldn't pray, meditate, dance, sing, or do ceremonies without a body. In Inka spirituality, we do not seek to transcend the body, but to inhabit it fully, opening ourselves to its wisdom every day.

The Power of the Breath

One of the best ways to fully inhabit our bodies is to reconnect with the breath. Our breath is intimately connected with Mama Huayra—the wind. When we connect with Mama Huayra, we are connecting with the director of our thoughts and our dreams. Have you ever noticed how when somebody is very scared, their breathing is different? They breathe quickly, and while they're panicking, they can't think straight. This points to an important truth: how we breathe is how we think. If you can control your breath, you can control your thoughts—you can calm yourself and purify your mind.

Many of my American friends like to do something they call breathwork. They are always asking me, "Jorge, do you do breathwork in your tradition?" Of course, I have to remind them that in the Andean world, we don't really like that word "work." The word *trabajo* comes from suffering—why would I want to suffer when I breathe? Instead, I explain that my connection to breath starts with gratitude to the Amazon and all the great forests of the earth. After all, this is where our oxygen comes from. Before we do breathing practices, we should start by saying thank you to the Amazon that we can breathe at all, and thank you that we are alive.

As in many indigenous traditions, Inka healing is centered around the breath. Quechua *paqos* and Aymara yatiris like my mother use the power of breath to expel heavy energies from the body and send them to Mother Earth for purification. We also use breath to blow light into coca leaves when we are making a k'intu offering, and to blow our prayers and gratitude into any other type of offering we are making. The breath carries your intention and your light; it expresses what you cannot even say in words. This is what makes the breath such a powerful vehicle for prayer.

Where I grew up near Lake Titicaca, the elevation was about 12,500 feet—enough to give you altitude sickness if you're visiting from far away. Up there, the air is thinner than at sea level, so knowing how to breathe deeply and calmly is very important, and can even mean the difference between life and death. My Aymara ancestors developed larger lungs and chest capacity to oxygenate their blood at high altitude—this is one more way in which we are one with our mountain environment.

The breath is our connection to all of life. Just as you are breathing in and out, so every living creature on earth is breathing in and out. All living beings share the same air; try as you might, you can never say, "This is *my* oxygen over here and *your* oxygen over there!"

Not only does breath connect living beings to one another, it also connects earthly beings to the divine. When we breathe in and out, we are exchanging energy with the universe. What kind of energy are you breathing in? What kind of energy are you breathing out? How does this change when you are in a state of love and light, versus when you feel tight, contracted, and upset?

Anytime you feel cut off from wisdom, from yachay, take a moment to check in with your breath. Pause and simply breathe for a few moments, allowing any fear that has entered your mind to be released. Ask Mama Huayra to carry this fear away. Work *with* the wind—with the earth and all its natural elements—to come back to a state of wisdom.

The Wisdom of the Earth

Just as we all have access to the wisdom and attunement of our bodies, we also have access to the wisdom of the earth—indeed, of the entire cosmos. Every mountain, every river, every flower possesses deep knowledge about how to live a good life. The mountains show us how to be strong and age gracefully; rivers teach us to flow; flowers show us how to draw energy out of the earth to provide beauty and spiritual nourishment for all. The wisdom of nature is available to us at all times, no matter where or who we are. We all live on this earth, in this universe, and we all have the power to pay attention to what's around us.

Many spiritual traditions around the world have a concept of initiation—a moment when you pass from a state of ignorance to wisdom, or childishness to maturity. These initiations often take place in nature. Among the wisdom keepers of the Andes, the word for this type of initiation is *karpay*. A karpay is a sacred compact between you and a specific place or energy. For example, in some Andean communities, the wisdom keepers will make a karpay with a certain mountain or Apu. This means they are establishing a relationship, asking that mountain to be their ally and walk with them, and in turn they will be a friend to the mountain.

Of course, everything that exists is already our ally and already supporting us. You don't need to make karpay with a certain mountain to receive that mountain's love and wisdom. The same is true of Father Sun and Mother Earth and with the rivers and the stars. Making karpay doesn't mean that you get special powers or special access to the energy of that being that you didn't have before; on the contrary, karpay is a way to remember and affirm the connection that's already there, and that has been there since the very moment you were born.

In Peru, we have all kinds of ceremonies for karpay. For example, the ceremony for karpay with the stars is very beautiful. Sitting under the stars with a *mesa*, or portable altar, the person doing karpay will sing, "*Hampe, hampe, hampe*: We call, we call, we call. Come, come, come, come."

Sure enough, when we bring our attention to the energy of the stars, we start to feel that energy within ourselves. It is in us and has always been with us—the only difference is that now we've made a sacred agreement to feel it and honor it. The more attention we pay, the more wisdom we receive; and the more wisdom we receive, the more grateful we are.

One wonderful way to access the wisdom of the earth is through walking. It often comes as a surprise to my American friends when I tell them that the Inka people never invented the wheel. Carts would have been unwieldly on the steep, bumpy mountainsides, and horses were unknown until the Spanish conquistador Francisco Pizarro brought them to Peru in 1531. Instead, the Inka people developed an incredible network of Qhapaq Ñan—trails paved with fitted stones. At the peak of the Inka civilization, there were almost ten thousand miles of Qhapaq Ñan winding their way through steep mountains and even carved into sheer cliff faces.

The Inkas traveled mainly on foot, using llamas as pack animals. Walking long distances meant they traveled far more slowly than we are accustomed to going today. By doing so, they maintained an intimate connection to the earth. Instead of whooshing past in a car or galloping along on a horse, they maintained their connection to Pachamama with every step. They had time to notice every plant, every cloud, and every trickle of water. Pausing at sacred sites was natural. Perhaps most important, they did not experience the jarring disconnect between body, mind, and spirit that affects many travelers in the modern, high-speed world.

The practice of walking can bring us back in sync with Mother Earth, healing the disconnect that comes from moving about too quickly. When we walk from one place to another, we are there the whole time. Not only that, but we use only the energy that our bodies can naturally provide, without relying on an artificial boost from gas or electricity. There is something magical about rediscovering this natural limit. It is amazing to hike to the top of a mountain, or walk from one side of a city to the other, or do the same in a wheelchair using your arms, and realize that it is *your body* that carried you this incredible distance.

In the modern world, we often forget just how incredible our bodies are. Of course, tools and machines can be wonderful for the convenience they afford us, and the ways they extend our bodies' natural power, but they can also lead us to forget just how much we are capable of on our own. To this day, many people in the Andes still use walking as their primary mode of transportation—a practice that is both practical in rural areas and important for maintaining a spiritual connection to the earth. Walking also maintains a link between time and space that our minds and bodies can readily understand, instead of collapsing it in a way that causes confusion to the spirit and restlessness to the body and mind. When we walk, we affirm our presence and participation in *this* time and *this* space, making the earth sacred with every step.

Around the world, the humble act of walking has long been associated with spiritual wisdom. When people in the Andes go on pilgrimage to sacred sites, they often walk, taking days or weeks to reach their destination. The long walks provide ample time for reflection—an opportunity for wisdom to bubble up from the Ukhu Pacha, filter down from Hanan Pacha, and be integrated in Kay Pacha. Even more than reaching the sacred site, it is the act of walking that builds yachay and changes the life of the pilgrim.

Life in Harmony

In the Andean tradition, the primary, living energy of the world is called kawsay. You may know this universal life force by another name, such as *chi*, *prana*, or *wakan*. It's the energy that animates all of creation. When kawsay flows freely, there is good health, flourishing, wisdom, and abundance. When it becomes blocked or stagnant, there is often disease, depression, ignorance, and deterioration. Every human being has the power to work with kawsay to create good health in our minds and bodies.

In the Quechua language, we have the expression *sumak kawsay*, which means "good life" or "life in harmony." This means creating a life that is healthy for our bodies, our minds, our communities, and for Mother Earth. As you grow in yachay, you will manifest sumak kawsay through your words, thoughts, and actions, doing your part to reflect the divine qualities of generosity, compassion, and love in your life here on earth. You will tap into the wisdom not only of your thinking mind, but of your body, the earth, and the cosmos, and this will lead you on a path of greater harmony for all beings.

Living as we do in an increasingly materialistic society, practicing sumak kawsay can be a little rebellious. It means rejecting the idea that we were put here on earth to accumulate endless personal riches, or to leave our families and communities in the dust as we race toward individual success. It means getting clear about what you really value—whether that's friendship, clean air and water, or plenty of time to make music and art—and then building your life around those values instead of the ones that are advertised to you by consumer culture. It means moving past self-centeredness to consider the best and highest good of all creatures alive on earth today, as well as future generations.

In 2008 and 2009, the governments of Ecuador and Bolivia incorporated sumak kawsay into their constitutions, declaring the peoples' right to a healthy environment, healthy community, and healthy body. These basic rights shouldn't be radical or controversial—after all, who doesn't want beautiful forests, happy neighborhoods, and healthy citizens?—but to the old pachakuti based on endless extraction and profit-seeking, these simple ideas can seem threatening.

As Children of the Sun, we know that a way of life based on fear, guilt, and greed will never lead us to true happiness. Knowing that the thinking mind alone will often lead us to make our choices based on these heavy energies, we can tap into the many other forms of wisdom that are available to us to balance things out. We can ask the earth, stars, and sun to support us with their wisdom, as well as our fellow creatures, other human beings, and the wisdom of our bodies and hearts.

Exercise: Healing Hands

Most of the time, we don't realize the power we have in our hands: the ability to feel and share warmth and light. Activating your healing hands is one of the most beautiful practices you can do to access your body's wisdom. When we activate our hands, we're really activating our intention and our ability to perceive refined energies or sámi.

First, hold your hands close together with the palms facing each other. Feel into the space between them. Now set your intention to activate healing energy. Count to seven out loud, speaking each number clearly. As you say each number, notice the energy building up between your palms. Feel the heat gathering there like invisible light. Notice if you feel any tingling or vibration.

Now slowly pull your palms away from each other until they are about six inches apart. Feel how the energy contained within them expands like a glowing ball. Bring this ball to the crown of your head and pour it down, letting the energy fill your entire body with light.

You can activate your hands in this way before conducting a ritual or ceremony, before engaging in any healing work, and to share light with others through touch.

Exercise: Ayni Breathing

Recall that the word *ayni* means "reciprocity." You can practice ayni breathing to engage in a sacred exchange with the universe, both giving and receiving energy.

First, find a quiet, comfortable space where you won't be disturbed for a few minutes. Ideally, you should do this practice outdoors, but you can also do it facing a window with a view of some trees, grass, or open sky. Stand or sit with your spine straight, and place your hands on your lower abdomen.

Begin to breathe slowly and deeply. As you inhale through your nose, imagine you are drawing in sámi. At the same time, you can visualize this sámi as pure, radiant light from the cosmos.

Now, when you exhale through your mouth, imagine you are expelling hucha. You can visualize this hucha as smoke or sludge, which you are giving back to Mother Earth to be purified.

Feel each breath as a sacred exchange: with every breath cycle, you are giving and receiving, giving and receiving. Remember, Mother Earth experiences hucha as a gift that she can easily turn into precious, fertile compost. You are not only receiving light, but helping Mother Earth to create more light and life in turn.

Chapter 9

The Wisdom of a Chakaruna

One of my favorite stories tells of a successful businessman who became a spiritual seeker. His whole life, he had done all the right things: study, get a good job, save money. But he felt that something was missing inside, and he didn't know what it was.

He heard that in the high mountains, there lived an elder who possessed deep yachay. He set out to find this elder, and when he arrived at his hut, he said, "Grandfather, can you teach me?"

"What is it that you want to learn?" said the elder.

The man replied, "I want to learn to expand my love."

He had heard that if you expanded your love enough, you could become a *tukuy munay niyo*: a master of love. When this happened, a hummingbird would appear over your head to drink the delicious nectar of love emanating there.

The elder said, "To expand your love, share your love with all your relations."

The man thanked the elder and hiked back home. He started sharing love with everyone he met. In the community, he was always the first to assist. When a family member or neighbor needed something, he would always show up.

And after a few months of this, he was feeling really good. Yet he found that he still felt some kind of emptiness inside.

He decided to go to the mountains again and visit the elder.

"Grandfather," he said, "Can you tell me what I am doing wrong here? Because, you know, I'm sharing my love, I'm helping a lot of people every day. But I still feel that emptiness inside."

This time, the elder said, "Tell me how much more you love *yourself* since last time you've been here."

The man was stunned. He said, "You never told me to love myself. You told me to share my love. That's what I was doing."

The elder replied, "If you don't love yourself, how do you know that what you are sharing is love?"

So the man went back home and practiced loving himself. He felt so much gratitude for his hands, his strong legs, which let him walk in the mountains, and his clever mind, which had allowed him to have so much success in business. He began to drop the heavy energy from his past, forgiving everything until he loved his life completely. He started doing despachos and other ceremonies to express his love for life.

After a while, he started to feel very happy. *I wonder if I've become a tukuy munay niyo*, he thought with excitement. *I'd better visit the grandfather to check.*

He goes back up the mountain and says, "Grandfather, look, I'm so happy. I finally understand what it means to love. Maybe I am a *tukuy munay niyo*, don't you think?"

And the elder replied, "I'm sorry, son. You are not there yet."

Now the man was a little bit frustrated. "How come? I haven't even told you about all of my experiences—the way I felt my inner sun light up when I was doing my ceremony the other day."

But the grandfather said, "You don't have to tell me. I know you are not there yet. Because when you are there, you don't have the question anymore. You don't need validation. You don't need a certificate. You don't need an initiation. You don't need anything."

In that moment, the man's eyes were opened. He saw that despite all the love and service he'd been practicing, he had not yet attained the wisdom of a chakaruna: the wisdom to know that the same light that burns in the sun and stars also burns in our hearts, and we don't need to climb a mountain to find it.

After thanking the elder, he went back home for the final time, picked up his shovel, and started tending his garden, which he'd been neglecting during his quest to become a tukuy munay niyo. He weeded his pumpkin patch and planted some beans, simply enjoying the beauty of the earth and feeling grateful for the life he'd been given. Just when he was about to go inside, he heard a faint sound above his head. It was a beautiful emerald hummingbird hovering just above him, drawn to the energy of his love.

The Blessings of the Hummingbird

In the Andean tradition, the hummingbird is seen as a divine messenger. The hummingbird is the only bird on earth that can hover, thanks to a ball-and-socket joint that lets its wings rotate in all directions. They are also the only birds on earth who can fly backward, and even upside down. The hummingbird moves its wings so fast, with such enthusiasm for life, that we cannot even count how many times per second its wings beat; to the human eye, it just looks like a blur. Is it any wonder the ancient Inkas saw this tiny bird as a magical being?

But the hummingbird has other qualities that make it special besides its unique physical structure. When a hummingbird comes to a flower, it doesn't destroy the flower. It just takes the nectar, the sweetness, and in return, it helps pollinate and bring more flowers to the world. This is a beautiful teaching of reciprocity—of ayni.

In the Andean tradition, we say that the hummingbird is a divine messenger from the cosmos. It appears because you have removed the blockages, you've released your resistance, you've opened all the petals, and you are ready to share your nectar; you are ready to share your sweetness; you are ready to share your beauty; you are ready to share your life.

But as the man in the story learned, before you can meet this cosmic messenger, you first have to try your own sweetness. You have to accept your own beauty, and accept that you are wise and that you are one with all life. When we do this, we become like the hummingbird. We experience all these great gifts of life without destroying the flower.

Some people think that becoming a chakaruna means accessing so-called higher states. Some talk about becoming a tukuy munay niyo—a master of love—or a *tukuy yachay niyo*—a master of wisdom, as if there is a hierarchy of love and wisdom you can climb, having special and unusual experiences along the way. Personally, I'm reluctant to speak about love, service, and wisdom in those terms, because it makes people think there is something to strive for, something to attain—and in their desire to attain these "special" things, they may chase after gurus and engage in spirituality contests, while forgetting the light that was within them all along.

I believe that there is only one love. There is no superior or inferior version; it is just love. Becoming a chakaruna doesn't require fancy initiations or bolts of lightning coming down from the sky. It just means waking up to your inner light, and letting the wisdom of that inner light inform everything you say and do.

Moving Through a Personal Pachakuti

In the introduction to this book, I explained the concept of a pachakuti: a period of time defined by a turning point or change. In Inka cosmology, global pachakutis take place roughly every five hundred years. However, we also undergo pachakutis in our own lives, during which our old way of living is no longer working, and we must use all the wisdom at our disposal to find a new and better way. If you've ever left a long-term relationship, changed careers, or undergone a significant transition such as the illness or death of a loved one, you know what it means to experience a pachakuti in your personal life.

Becoming a chakaruna often means going through an intense pachakuti during which you must shed old habits, beliefs, values, and identities. Perhaps your life thus far has been focused on the modern, materialistic definition of success. Maybe you were brought up to believe that the word *family* only refers to your parents, siblings, and other close relatives, that the middle world is the only reality to which human beings have access, or that humans are the only agents of consciousness in the universe. Transitioning to a new worldview that includes a sacred cosmos infused with life can be a great adventure—and quite a disruption to your ordinary life.

Often, our first response to a pachakuti is resistance. We have a stirring of inner wisdom letting us know it's time for a change, but we try to talk ourselves out of it, sternly reminding ourselves of all the "good" reasons to stay in the same pattern. We say, *But I'm making good money* or *My parents really want me to marry him*. We use our rational minds to overrule our inner wisdom, thinking it will keep us safe from all the unknowns that would come by making a big change.

Putting up this kind of resistance often feels like the right thing to do. Yet it comes from the hucha of fear. When we engage in these self-protective mechanisms, we forget that we are part of a larger whole. We forget that Mother Earth and Father Sun will always be there for us, no matter where we go or what we choose. We focus on the seeming problems and obstacles we perceive in Kay Pacha, while avoiding whatever's speaking to us from deep within Ukhu Pacha, or calling to us from Hanan Pacha.

Engaging wholeheartedly with a pachakuti in your life means tapping into all three realms and embracing the wisdom they share. It's also important to check in with potential sources of fear. Does your resistance come from an unprocessed trauma deep in your past? Do you feel overwhelmed by obstacles and logistical challenges of the everyday world? Are you afraid of listening to your higher wisdom in case it tells you to do something scary, radical, or out of line with who you have thus far believed yourself to be?

Next, it's important to open yourself up to fully receiving the wisdom of the three realms. When you sit in silent meditation or contemplation, does your intuition send out messages from deep within your subconscious mind? When you're going about your daily life, do you experience frequent signs and coincidences that all seem to be pointing in the same direction? When you look at your life from the perspective of a condor, what bigger picture do you see emerging?

Finally, successfully transitioning through a personal pachakuti means learning to trust the wisdom you receive from all three realms, without dismissing or minimizing any of them, or engaging in wishful thinking. In this example, yachay requires hearing and seeing things clearly, without ignoring inconvenient truths or fabricating experiences you merely wish to be true. It means stepping into your new reality exactly as it is, without adding or removing anything. When you can do this, you can harvest the full gifts of your pachakuti, sharing your newfound wisdom with all of creation.

Opening the Portal

Back in the 1990s, I made a discovery that initiated a pachakuti in my own life and set me on my path of becoming a chakaruna. For weeks, I kept having intense dreams about dramatic formations of pink stone. When I asked an elder shaman about these visions, he simply told me, "Follow the feeling."

I began to search for the place I had seen in my dreams, following my instincts as I hiked around Lake Titicaca. One day, I was out just after sunrise. This is the perfect time to visit sacred places: when Father Sun is low in the sky, casting shadows that reveal the true nature of the stones. The entire area was bathed in soft, clear light, engulfed in a mystical cloak even though the highway was only a few steps away. The sandstones glowed a luminous pink, and the rock clusters on the flat landscape felt vibrantly alive.

Following my intuition, I was led to a large natural pink sandstone wall, approximately eighteen feet wide and twenty-one feet high. A mysterious doorway cut into the wall caught my attention. The doorway was cut about twelve inches deep into the stone. Immediately, I was filled with reverence. This was the place I had seen in my dream—but what was it?

As I approached, I sensed that this doorway was connected to another dimension.

As is our Andean tradition, I asked permission of the spirit guardians of the place before getting any closer. Then I stood inside the doorway, stretching out my arms so that my fingertips brushed each side. It seemed as if the doorway was made to fit exactly a person my size. It felt like I had penetrated deep inside myself and deep inside the natural rock structure simultaneously.

The next thing I knew, I was seeing floating colors and getting chills. This was followed by an intense feeling of warmth. I saw an iridescent white cloth engulfing my body and had a series of visions unlike anything I'd experienced before. In my most meaningful vision, I saw the back of a man carrying a golden disc walking through the doorway and disappearing into the wall. I don't know how long I stood there in this state of bliss and humility. Gently, the doorway released me, and I stepped back, filled with gratitude and awe.

When I reflected on my vision later, I realized that it was related to the legendary Golden Disc of the Inkas. According to ancient stories, this disc was not merely an object of beauty but a scientific instrument of great power that could cause earthquakes or teleport Inka priests anywhere in the universe. When the Spanish conquerors arrived, the Inkas hid the Golden Disc, and it has never been found since.

For a while, I shared my discovery with only a few close friends. But a few years later, I started taking travelers to visit the portal. When I first invited people to the doorway, I knew of no name for it. I was curious and asked many local people about existing names. I found that an ancient traditional name for the portal was Willka Uta, meaning the House of Divinity, the House of the Sun. Another name was Altarani, meaning the place with the altar. The name that the Spanish used to deter people from visiting this place was the Devil's Doorway.

When I reflect on the moment when I first stood in the stone portal, I realize that this experience was an expanding bridge for me into other dimensions and other realities. Up until that point, I was still resisting the understanding that life consists of the spiritual, not only the physical and material. After my experience at Willka Uta, I could no longer deny that this was true.

What I have learned through my years of guiding others to this sacred portal is that we do not need to travel to Lake Titicaca to find our own mystical doorway. Each of us carries within our heart a portal even more powerful than the one carved in stone. This inner doorway connects us directly to the light of Father Sun, to the love of Mother Earth, and to the wisdom of the cosmos.

Whenever we tap into our inner sun, we are standing at the threshold of our own House of Divinity. This simple practice—love without fear—is the key that opens our inner doorway to all dimensions. In our Andean tradition, we believe that our heart is where the light of our inner sun resides. It is the meeting place where Pachatata and Pachamama—the Divine Father and Divine Mother—connect within us. As we clear the heavy energies that cloud this inner light, our heart becomes a living portal through which we can access all the wisdom of our ancestors, all the love of creation, and all the power of our true divine nature.

When pilgrims come to visit the physical portal at Lake Titicaca, what they are really seeking is a reminder of the portal they already possess. The stone doorway is just a reflection, a mirror showing us what lies within. This is why some people weep when they stand there—not because they cannot pass through the physical stone, but because for a moment they remember the infinite possibilities that exist within their own hearts.

Exercise: Hummingbird Practice

Here is a practice inspired by the hummingbird to help you connect with your inner sweetness and share it with the world.

First, find a quiet place where you can be undisturbed. If possible, do this practice outside where you can see Father Sun, feel Mother Earth beneath your feet, and maybe even see some flowers.

Begin by greeting Father Sun. Open your arms wide facing east, letting the light touch your heart. Feel the rays of light entering through your eyes, your skin, awakening your inner sun.

Place your right hand on your heart, opening yourself to love, and your left hand on your solar plexus, closing the door of fear. Feel how the light in your heart expands, making a bubble of light around you.

Now bring your attention to your crown chakra, the top of your head. Imagine it is opening like a beautiful flower in full bloom. Feel all your petals opening, one by one.

As your crown opens, feel the sweetness, the nectar inside you. This is your light, your love, your wisdom. Feel how sweet it is, how beautiful. Taste your own nectar, your own sweetness.

Now imagine the cosmic hummingbird is coming to you, hovering above your crown, attracted by your sweetness. Feel how this cosmic hummingbird is taking your nectar, your sweetness, and sharing it with the world, helping to pollinate more flowers, more hearts.

Feel how you are in service to life, not by working hard, but by being who you truly are: a being of light, of love, of wisdom. Stay in this state as long as you wish, feeling the joy of sharing your sweetness without depleting yourself, without destroying your flower.

Exercise: Chakaruna Karpay

In this exercise, I invite you to create your own ceremony to affirm and celebrate your commitment to living as a chakaruna: a bridge person in service to all of creation. In this unique karpay, you can connect with the energies of any places, beings, or energies that can help and inspire you in a life of sacred service.

First, identify any places, beings, or natural forces with which you would like to make karpay. These might include:

- Mountains that have special meaning to you
- Bodies of water that have nourished you

- Ancestors who have inspired your path
- Teachers who have shared their wisdom with you
- Animals that have appeared as messengers in your life
- Stars or constellations that were present at your birth
- Trees that have offered shelter and strength

Remember, these energies are *already* supporting you. This karpay is not to gain something new, but to remember and acknowledge the connection that already exists.

Next, create a simple altar or sacred space for your ceremony. This might include:

- A textile or cloth to represent the weaving of worlds

- Stones or crystals to anchor energies
- Flowers or plants to honor Mother Earth
- Water in a beautiful vessel to represent Mama Qocha
- A candle or other fire element to represent Mama Nina
- Images or symbols of the energies you wish to connect with
- Personal objects that represent your commitment to love, service, and wisdom

When you are ready, open your space by lighting incense, greeting the four directions, and cleansing your energy field in any way that feels meaningful to you. Ask that any hucha or heavy energy preventing you from being a clear bridge be released to Mother Earth for transformation.

Next, call upon each of the energies you've chosen to witness and support your commitment. For example, "Beloved Apu, I acknowledge your presence in my life. I recognize your wisdom, strength, and endurance. I ask that you walk with me as I serve as a bridge between worlds." Take your time calling on each energy one by one and sincerely expressing your gratitude as well as any specific requests you have.

When you have finished, place your hands on your heart and speak aloud your intention to live as a chakaruna. For example: "I commit myself to being a bridge person, bringing together all the gifts of the upper world, the inner world, and the middle world. I offer my unique gifts in service to all life. I commit to letting the light of love, service, and wisdom flow through me."

Now simply pause. Open yourself to receiving the energy of all the beings and forces you've invoked. Feel the energy flowing into your crown, your heart, and throughout your body. Know that this energy has always been available to you.

Anchor this energy by creating a triangle with your fingers over your heart. Feel yourself coming into a state of sacred agreement with all that exists.

Finish your ceremony by offering something back to each of the energies you've invoked. This might be a k'intu, a song, a dance, a prayer, or simply your heartfelt thanks. Remember that all relationships follow the principle of ayni: you receive and you give.

Finally, consider how you will honor this commitment in your daily life. What small practice can you do each day to remember your role as a chakaruna? It might be greeting the sun each morning, planting trees with your neighbors, or spending a few moments in silence connecting with your inner wisdom before making decisions.

Remember, this commitment is not something you make once and then it's finished. It is something you renew daily through your actions, your awareness, and your willingness to serve from the heart. Each time you greet the sun, each time you speak from love instead of fear, each time you offer kindness where there was harshness, you are living your commitment as a chakaruna.

May your path as a bridge person bring joy to you and to all beings.

Conclusion

When friends part ways in the Andes, they do not say goodbye, but *tupananchiskama*—until we meet again. This is a reflection of the fact that we will all meet each other again in the form of energy and light, even if our paths never cross again in Kay Pacha. When we practice munay, llankay, and yachay, we affirm our essential connection to this light that infuses all that exists, binding us to one another in mysterious ways.

By this point, I hope you understand that munay, llankay, and yachay are not separate but form one unified whole. Like the three sides of a triangle, they support and strengthen one another, creating a foundation of peace, stability, and harmony in our lives. When we cultivate this sacred triangle, we can harness the warmth of munay, the generosity of llankay, and the discernment of yachay. We do not have to wait for special permission to work with these energies, but we can all begin right now, today, to do our part in the new pachakuti.

As we come to the end of this book, I invite you to continue tending to this triangle of light everywhere you go. Remember that all expressions of life, from the tiniest pebble to the tallest mountain, manifest the wisdom of the cosmos. Remember that everything that exists is in service, whether we understand the nature of that service or not.

Most important, remember that the best decision you will ever make is to love. When we love, we awaken to the light that flows through all things. The more we love, the more light we see, until everything reveals itself as an expression of the divine. We see the beauty of Pachamama. We feel the warmth of Father Sun. We know that we are never alone, but that threads of light connect us all.

Tupananchiskama—until we meet again.

Glossary of Quechua and Aymara Terms

ayllu: Community or extended family unit in the Andes that forms the basic social structure; includes not just blood relatives but also the mountains, animals, plants, and all expressions of life.

Amaru: The sacred two-headed serpent who represents wisdom and transformation; associated with Ukhu Pacha (the inner world).

Apukuna/Apus: Mountain spirits; powerful multidimensional beings considered to be silent watchers, protectors, and masters.

ayni: Reciprocity; the sacred exchange of energy that maintains harmony and balance in all relationships.

camac/camay: To animate or infuse with life; a camac is that which provides sacred energy.

chakaruna: Bridge person; someone who helps others cross from one state of consciousness to another, forming bridges between different worlds.

Hanan Pacha: The upper or celestial world; realm of light beings, spiritual teachers, and the divine self.

hucha: Heavy energy that doesn't come from love; often manifests as fear, resentment, anger, or shame.

Inka: From *Inti* (sun) and *kana* (clear, transparent light); refers both to a state of consciousness and the civilization that flourished in the Andes.

Inti: The sun or sun energy; refers not just to the physical sun but to the energy that transmits cosmic codes through refined frequencies.

kana: Clear, pure, transparent light that comes as a ray from Father Sun.

kawsay: Life force energy; the primary, living energy of the world.

Kay Pacha: The middle world; our everyday reality, the here and now.

k'intu: An offering consisting of three coca leaves (or other natural elements) used in ceremonies to release heavy energies or send prayers.

llankay: Sacred service or work; one of the three pillars of Inka spirituality.

Mama Nina: Mother Fire; the feminine spirit of fire and transformation.

Mama Qocha: Mother Ocean or Mother Sea; the feminine spirit of water.

Mama Wayra: Mother Wind; the feminine spirit of air and breath.

minka: Collective work for the benefit of the community; combines service with celebration and joy.

munay: Unconditional love; one of the three pillars of Inka spirituality.

nayra: The past; also means "eye," indicating that we see with the past.

Pachamama: The Divine Mother, Cosmic Mother; often translated simply as Mother Earth, but encompasses much more.

Pachacamac/Pachatata: The Divine Father, Cosmic Father.

Pachakuti: A great turning or transformation; a time when old ways die out and new ways of living begin.

Qhapaq Ñan: The network of trails and roads built by the Inka throughout their realm.

sámi: Refined energy that comes from love; the food that nourishes the soul.

sumak kawsay: Good life or life in harmony; creating a life that is healthy for our bodies, communities, and Mother Earth.

Tawantinsuyu: "The Realm of the Four Parts"; the name the Inka people used for their civilization.

tinkuy: The coming together of two seemingly distinct or opposing energies; a sacred meeting point.

Ukhu Pacha: The inner world or lower world; realm of the subconscious mind where memories and past experiences are stored.

yachay: Wisdom or divine knowledge; one of the three pillars of Inka spirituality.

yatiri: Traditional healer.

About the Author

Jorge Luis Delgado, an Inka by birth and heritage, walks the path of the chakaruna. His passion is to bring authentic Inka heritage, spiritual traditions and handcrafts to worldwide attention. He considers the oral tradition, taught in the different Inka communities, to be his ever-expanding higher education.

San Antonio, TX
www.hierophantpublishing.com